HOW TO LEARN GOLF

The First Complete Guide to Golf Instruction Based on Exclusive Sessions with the Game's Top Teaching Pros

Harry Hurt III

ATRIA BOOKS
New York London Toronto Sydney Singapore

Hurt, Harry.
    How to learn golf / Harry Hurt III.
        p.cm.
    Includes bibliographical references.
    ISBN 0-7434-1726-7 (alk. paper)
        1. Golf—Study and teaching. I. Title: How to learn golf. II. Title.

 GV962.5 . H87 2002
 796.352'3—dc21

                                        2001059816

First Atria Books hardcover printing May 2002

10 9 8 7 6 5 4 3 2 1

ATRIA BOOKS is a trademark of Simon & Schuster, Inc.

For information regarding special discounts for bulk purchases, please contact
Simon & Schuster Special Sales at 1-800-456-6798 or business@simonandschuster.com

Printed in the U.S.A.

*For W.H.H., A.B.H.,
and W.R.H.*

ACKNOWLEDGMENTS

The author owes special thanks to all the golf instructors mentioned in this book, and to the following people: Sam Walsh (photographs), Jon Rizzi, Bart Richardson, Stan Rumbough, Barbara Hearst, Victor Ayad, Shannon Wynne, Arthur Dodge, Rick Teischgraber, Scott Bertrand Sr., Scott Bertrand Jr., Jaimie Roggero Carbone, Dick Clark, Tina Bradley, William Beatty, Will Katz, Anne O. Katz, Dr. Dana Harper, Techla Harper, John Brown, John Tolbert, Charles Grubb, Paul H. Livingston, Barbara Smith, Patricia Birch, William R. Hurt, Dana Hurt, Harrison Hurt, Alison Hurt, Judith Curr, Ian Jackman, Luke Dempsey, Suzanne O'Neill, and Mark Reiter.

CONTENTS

PREFACE:
Golf Is a Game of Hope

If you go to a public or private golf course anywhere in America, chances are you will find the vast majority of golfers in the same states. Some will be in a state of confusion. Others will be in states of embarrassment, frustration, or despair. Precious few will be in states of joy or rapture. Golf is a game of hope. We all want to play better than we did the last time out, even if we haven't practiced since. Most of all, golf is a game that's supposed to be fun. But the nation's links are teeming with hookers and slicers muttering all sorts of four-letter words other than *golf* and *hope*. And judging by the expressions on many of their faces, they aren't having a whole lot of fun at it.

Ironically, average golfers are even more likely to be discombobulated if they are taking or have taken golf lessons, especially if they have sought help from more than one instructor. America's teaching professionals often seem to be operating on entirely different wavelengths, offering diametrically opposite advice. Pro number

one tells you to control the golf swing with your hands and arms, and let your body respond. Pro number two tells you to control the golf swing with your body, and let your hands and arms respond. Pro number three says you should stroke your putts on a line path straight back and straight through with a pendulum motion. Pro number four insists you should stroke your putts on a semicircular arc path like a swinging gate.

The hope of playing better, meanwhile, remains nothing more than a pipe dream. During the past two decades, we have witnessed the introduction of high-tech equipment ranging from titanium-headed drivers to solid-core balls that offer both more distance and more control. These innovations have no doubt benefited already proficient golfers. On the PGA Tour, average driving distances have increased more than ten yards in the last ten years, and long-standing tournament scoring records are being broken with increasing frequency. But according to United States Golf Association statistics, the average handicaps of male and female amateur golfers have not declined by a single stroke in thirty years, a fact apologists for the golf instruction establishment try to explain away by pointing out that the total population of golfers has grown threefold and that architects have been making golf courses more difficult and more penal.

No wonder the current golf boom is teetering on the brink of a bust. Between 1970 and 1990, the number of people playing golf in the United States more than tripled from 8 million to an all-time

peak of 27.8 million, according to the National Golf Foundation. But over the past decade, even as estimates of potential participation or "latent demand" have zoomed toward the 50 million mark, actual participation has declined by 4 percent to a current level of about 26.4 million. While the phenomenal exploits of Tiger Woods have driven up television ratings for PGA Tour golf, they have not staunched an ongoing attrition in the number of people playing the game. In 1999, an estimated 3 million people took up golf for the first time, but roughly 3 million others quit.

According to a recent *Wall Street Journal* report, most people who quit golf cite at least one of four principal reasons. First, golf is expensive, particularly compared to recreational sports such as tennis, bowling, or swimming. Second, golf is time-consuming. It typically takes four and a half hours, and often over five hours, to complete a round at most publicly accessible courses during peak months. Third, golf is intimidating. Even veteran PGA Tour pros confide that they feel nauseous prior to competing in an important tournament. And finally, golf is difficult to play well with any measure of consistency, as pro basketball star Michael Jordan, one of the world's greatest athletes, will readily attest.

It is my belief that most of the blame for the problems presently stunting the growth of golf lies not with the people who are trying to learn the game but with the people who are teaching it, including the vast majority of professional golf instructors and the

golf media who publish and broadcast instructional information. Let me hasten to add that I count myself among the guilty parties.

My inspiration and qualifications for writing this book stem from the fact that I am a kind of missing link between teaching pros and their pupils, the golf media and the average player. I am both a dispenser and a consumer of golf instruction, a golf writer who has also been a touring pro, a teaching pro, and an inveterate duffer. I know what it is like to try to learn golf from scratch, what it is like to quit the game, and what it is like to try to relearn the game after an extended layoff, because I have done all three.

I first started playing golf in Texas at age ten and competed in junior, high school, collegiate, and amateur golf tournaments against future PGA Tour stars such as Ben Crenshaw and Bruce Lietzke. At the age of nineteen I quit the golf team at Harvard, sold my clubs, and embarked on a career as a journalist and author of books about subjects other than golf. After a twenty-five-year hiatus from the game, I launched a golfing comeback, which I chronicled in my 1997 book *Chasing the Dream: A Midlife Quest for Fame and Fortune on the Pro Golf Circuit.*

In the course of researching *Chasing the Dream,* I competed on professional mini-tours, experienced the trauma of failing to make the cut in the first stage of PGA Tour Qualifying School, and won a pro tournament on the 40+ Tour of Florida. I subsequently passed the Playing Ability Test prerequisite for membership in the PGA of

America, the organization that certifies most of the nation's club pros and teaching pros, and became a contributor to leading golf publications. I am presently editor at large of the magazine *Travel & Leisure Golf,* for which I write a regular column on golf instruction.

My research for this book has taken me down a road not traveled by the average golfer or golf writer, or by the average touring pro or teaching pro, for that matter. Over a twenty-four-month period, I took lessons from twenty-one of the nation's leading golf instructors. My list of mentors includes all of the top ten teaching pros in America, as selected in a poll of their peers conducted by *Golf Digest* in 2000. In order of ranking, they are: David Leadbetter, Butch Harmon, Jim McLean, Hank Haney, Rick Smith, Jim Flick, Dave Pelz, Chuck Cook, Bob Toski, and Jimmy Ballard.

I have also been tutored by Mike Adams, Dick Harmon, Michael Hebron, Darrell Kestner, David Lee, Paul Marchand, Randy Smith, and Mitchell Spearman, all of whom are on *Golf Magazine's* list of top one hundred teaching pros, as well as by such up-and-coming instructors as Bruce Davidson, Eben Dennis, and Eden Foster. And I have reviewed the instructional advice I received as a junior golfer from the late Harvey Penick and the distinguished Texas teaching pro Jackson Bradley, the man who taught me to play golf starting at age ten.

In a metaphorical sense, I have also made a return trip to Harvard by simultaneously studying the sports psychology and sociology

of golf. It so happens that psychology and sociology were my college majors, so I consider myself one of the rare individuals who's actually gotten some practical use from a liberal arts degree. My academic training has helped me apply the insights of experts on individual and group behavior, such as the Harvard psychology professor Robert F. Bales, and to gain a better understanding of the approaches of sports psychologists Dr. Rick Jensen, Dr. Phil Lee, and Dr. Bob Rotella, with whom I consulted in researching this book.

I know of no one else who has run such a comprehensive instructional gauntlet, with the possible exception of Peter Kessler. As host of *Academy Live* on the Golf Channel, Kessler played ringmaster to a circus parade of instructors that includes most, if not all, of the teaching pros listed above. In his case, the results have been rather counterproductive. "I was a three handicap . . . in 1995," Kessler noted in a speech at the PGA of America's 2000 Teaching and Coaching Summit. "I'm now the worst nine that ever lived. . . . We figured out I've only had 39,412 tips so far on *Academy Live* since 1995, almost all of which I can remember just before impact."

I can certainly empathize with Kessler. I have suffered my share of sorrows from overcoaching, so-called paralysis by analysis. And after taking so many lessons from so many different instructors for the sake of research (something I strongly advise you not to do for the sake of your sanity), I am only now beginning to relocate my own swing. But I also have a new appreciation of the positive

effects a master teacher can have when your game goes awry or you fail to achieve your full potential. The most eloquent testimony is the fact that in addition to helping some of the greatest players of all time, including Fred Couples, Ernie Els, Nick Faldo, Lee Janzen, Tom Kite, Davis Love III, Phil Mickelson, Jack Nicklaus, Greg Norman, Nick Price, the late Payne Stewart, Hal Sutton, and Tiger Woods, the top-ranked teaching pros featured in this book have also helped thousands of average golfers. And me.

At the same time, I remain highly critical of the culture of contemporary golf instruction, particularly instruction aimed at the mass market. I am not alone. In his book *The Only Golf Lesson You'll Ever Need,* top-ten teaching pro Hank Haney expresses an opinion that is widely shared but seldom publicly uttered by his peers at the peak of the profession. "It pains me to say this, but the average golf instructor in this country isn't that good," Haney declares. "Not only that, there isn't much difference in the way most teachers teach. Until you get to the top instructors, that is. Then there's a huge difference. Which is why they are the best; they stand out from the crowd. But there isn't much [difference] between very good and poor [teachers]."

To put it politely, the current state of golf instruction is in a state of confusion not unlike that which befuddles average golfers. There are more than 25,000 members and apprentices of the PGA of America, and you can be sure that 25,000 members and appren-

tices of any organization cannot be of equal competence and talent. In recent years, the PGA has instituted its Playing Ability Test, a fairly rigorous Golf Professional Training Program, and an advanced specialty certification program in teaching, which all promise to improve the quality and qualifications of its membership. But even the most acclaimed PGA teaching pros do not share a common philosophy, and few offer an historical or methodological overview of golf instruction for their pupils. The confusion is only compounded by the fact that the majority of golf instructors speak of "the" golf swing or "the" putting stroke in monolithic terms, as if there were only one way to swing a club or stroke a putt.

The golf media, meanwhile, disseminate instructional material in tip-of-the-month-club fashion. One month, the vogue is to hold the golf club with a "strong" left-hand grip to cure your slice. The next month, the vogue is to hold the club with a relatively "weak" left-hand grip in the interests of greater control and accuracy. It is not uncommon to find one article in a leading magazine that advocates using your legs and hips to generate power, and another article in the very same magazine that claims quick hands and "quiet" legs are the real keys to generating power. Perhaps the only constant is the continuing barrage of advice, for if the instructional magazines and television shows were ever to run out of new tips, they would effectively go out of business.

In fairness, consumers of golf instruction must share some of

the responsibility for promoting the tip-of-the-month mentality in the golf media and among teaching pros. Being human, many golfers are impatient to improve their games by the fastest and easiest means possible. One such means is "buying" improvement in the form of the latest high-tech equipment. Another is demanding short-term fixes for their swing flaws rather than long-term solutions, Band-Aids rather than lasting cures. Golf instructors and the golf media respond by providing what the market and the golfing masses seem to demand. Michael Hebron, a top-ranked teaching pro who has coached the likes of former U.S. Open champion Jerry Pate and former Masters champion Ian Woosnam, believes that this vicious cycle is at the root of the problems that plague golf instruction.

"Coaches in other sports are more mentors than gurus with secrets," Hebron observed in an interview after one of our lessons. "I believe that if the culture of golf instruction were geared less to communication of 'how-to' information, people would learn faster. People are always trying to 'fix' their slices or 'fix' their swings. But they should be trying to develop a body of core knowledge they can use to help themselves learn. They should be looking for an anchor, not a life preserver."

This book aims to clear up the confusion surrounding golf instruction and the process of learning golf with a straightforward, unbiased presentation of core knowledge in historical context. My goal is not to teach you how to swing a club or how to stroke a putt.

Rather, it is to identify and describe the leading methods and the available instructional options, and to provide the information you need to make informed choices so you can learn how to swing a club and how to stroke a putt with the methods and the instructors best suited to you and your own golfing goals.

An argument can be made that nothing is inherently wrong with a golfer seeking short-term fixes or tips. Haney himself points out that no one, not even Tiger Woods, has a "perfect swing." Every golfer, PGA Tour pros and rank beginners alike, has at least two or more compensations in his swing that critics might describe as flaws in comparison to an abstract ideal of perfection or a computer model. Impatience aside, few golfers are willing or able to spend hundreds of hours on the practice range overhauling their games. As a result, most golf instruction is what teaching pros call "error correction" rather than "swing development." But even if you are trying to fix compensations, you need to do so within the context of an overall game plan so you don't fix the wrong compensations and revert to square one again.

If you really want to be successful in learning how to hit the little white ball, it is important to see the big picture. There is no such thing as "the" golf swing or "the" putting stroke. In fact, there are at least three major types of golf swings and three major types of putting strokes, and innumerable permutations, combinations, subtypes, and hybrids of each. Like painting, playing golf is as much art

as science. The same goes for teaching golf and learning golf. Along with being products of different time periods, Leonardo da Vinci and Pablo Picasso represented entirely different schools of painting. Similarly, Butch Harmon, the scion of an illustrious American golf family who coaches Tiger Woods, ascribes to an entirely different theory of how to swing a golf club and how to stroke a putt than South African–born master instructor David Leadbetter or short-game guru Dave Pelz.

"Always bear in mind that one swing does not fit all, and that you must build your theories and swing keys around your own needs and requirements," Leadbetter, who is known as the most method-oriented of the top teaching pros, writes in *The Fundamentals of Hogan,* his recently published book about the legendary Ben Hogan. "That's what Hogan did, and it's what every golfer at his or her own level should do."

It is also important to bear in mind that golf swings and golf instruction have been transformed by advances in technology and golf club design. During the hickory-shaft and steel-shaft eras, many top players employed a form of the so-called small-muscle swing, which relies on the small muscles of the hands, arms, and knees for power and control. With the introduction of graphite shafts, the modern big-muscle swing, which relies on the big muscles of the torso, and the postmodern mixed-muscle swing have become the rage. All three types of swings have their advantages and disadvan-

tages. But a golfer needs to know the difference, then pick the most suitable method and stick with it under the guidance of an instructor who can teach it effectively. If you're trying to make big-muscle swings but your pro is a proponent of the small-muscle method, or vice versa, your efforts at improvement will inevitably be doomed before you hit the first ball off the practice range.

The overall organization of the chapters that follow is in keeping with one of the tenets of the teaching philosophy outlined in *Harvey Penick's Little Red Book: Lessons and Teachings from a Lifetime in Golf*—to wit, "Golf should be learned starting at the cup and progressing backward toward the tee." That makes strategic sense given that the goal of the game is getting the ball into the hole. It also makes sense in athletic and cognitive terms. By starting with the shortest of swings, putting strokes, and then advancing to full swings, you can gradually stretch both your muscles and your mind, and get an overview of how the various facets of the game fit together.

Along the way, you will also gain a basic understanding of the major putting, full-swing, and short-game methods, and the philosophies of the leading instructors associated with each of them. Appendix A lists America's top ten teaching pros and nineteen additional names of distinction; lesson rates, contact information, and a brief biographical profile accompany each listing. Appendices B and C provide lists of questions to ask yourself and your prospective instructor before taking a golf lesson, while appen-

dix D provides offers a few words of advice about equipment and club fitting. "Sources" suggests books that explore particular subject areas in more depth.

Of course, as Penick himself would surely remind us, you can't "take dead aim" on improving your golf game before you know who is holding the golf club and why. Great instructors don't teach golf to people, they help people learn golf. That's where you, the reader, come in. The opening chapter will show you how to help yourself in the learning process by mapping out a plan to improve your game. It offers both diagnostic and prescriptive means to determine what type of golfer you really are, how to set realistic goals for improvement, and what to consider when choosing what type of instructional approach and type of instructor may be right for you.

My hope is that this book will slay, or at least disable, two of the demons that are prompting people to quit golf or refrain from playing golf—the intimidation factor and the difficulty factor. Reducing these factors may also indirectly reduce the expense of golf, and the time the average round of golf consumes. If you can learn to play better, you will save money, if only by virtue of losing fewer golf balls per round. Likewise, you are also likely to play faster; you will spend less time chasing after wayward balls in woods and water hazards, and less time standing over each shot running through a mental checklist of superfluous swing thoughts. Best of all, you are almost certain to have more fun—and that's what playing the game of golf is really all about.

1 KNOW YOURSELF:
Making a Plan to Improve Your Game

All golfers are divided into two types—hookers and slicers.

Sure, just about everyone has hit a golf ball straight at some point. But it doesn't happen very often. Not even if you're among the top tour professionals in the world. And especially not if you're an amateur. Each of us has a tendency to hit the ball in one of two directions, either left or right. That tendency forms the essence of our individual golfing personalities, and it has profound implications for how we should go about improving our golf games.

It's easy enough to determine whether you're a hooker or a slicer. All you have to do is watch the prevailing direction in which most of your shots curve. If, as sometimes happens, you tend to hit your iron shots in one direction and your drives in the opposite direction, the curvature of your drives, particularly your bad drives, is definitive. Drivers offer the purest test of prevailing direction because they have less loft than irons, and as a result, impart less of the backspin that helps make balls fly straight.

The odds are almost overwhelming that the prevailing direction of your shots is to the right, which means you're a slicer. Although there has been no formal statistical survey, veteran golf instructors report that well over 85 percent of their students are chronic banana ballers. True hookers, as opposed to those of us who occasionally pull shots to the left, are a rare breed. But hookers often are or have the potential to be better players than their counterparts because they have demonstrated the ability to release the clubface through impact. As Harvey Penick observed in his *Little Red Book,* a slicer must learn to hook the ball before he can learn to hit the ball straight. (Note: If you are a left-hander, simply reverse these directional dictums—your hooks curve to the right; your slices curve to the left.)

Hookers and slicers are usually best advised to take opposite tacks in almost everything, including their choice of swing methods, as we'll see in the chapters ahead. But regardless of whether you hit your shots to the left or to the right, your starting point on the road to playing better golf is the same: if you want to make lasting improvements in your game, you have to begin by mapping out an effective learning program. And the key to that is to know yourself.

Both hookers and slicers have two main instructional approaches from which to choose. One is **error correction.** As the term implies, error correction focuses on a specific swing flaw or problem that needs fixing right away. The second approach is **swing development.** Here

the focus is on building or overhauling your golf swing from top to bottom. Each approach has its pros and cons. Error correction can often produce immediate, visible improvements in your ball flight, but it is by definition short-term in nature, more of a Band-Aid than a lasting cure. Swing development aims to make lasting improvements, but it can be complex, frustrating, and require considerable time and money.

Which instructional approach—error correction or swing development—is right for you? The answer depends entirely on who you are.

In fields such as science and medicine, the best researchers typically start by asking a series of probing questions about the subject they are researching. That's a good approach in golf, as well. Unfortunately, it is seldom practiced by the average golfer or the average golf instructor. But several top-ranked teaching pros, among them Mike Adams, Hank Haney, Butch Harmon, David Leadbetter, Jim McLean, Rick Smith, and Mitchell Spearman, endeavor to gather relevant background information on their students, either through formal written questionnaires, informal conversation, and/or on-site observation and exercises.

Here is a composite list of eighteen questions first-rate teaching pros might ask before giving you a lesson. They are also the kind of questions you should ask yourself before taking a lesson.

Eighteen Questions to Ask Yourself
Before Taking a Golf Lesson

1   How long have you been playing golf?

2   What is your present handicap?

3   What is the lowest your handicap has been?

4   What is your occupation?

5   How often do you practice and play golf?

6   How much money are you willing to spend on improving
     your game?

7   How much more time are you willing to spend on improving
     than you do now?

8   Are you looking to overhaul your golf game or simply to
     fix a specific fault?

9   What instructors and/or golf schools have you taken
     lessons from?

10   What are the strengths and weaknesses of your golf game?

11   What is your age?

12   Do you have any physical handicaps or injuries?

13 What is the state of your overall body flexibility and range of motion?

14 Do you have long, short, or average-length arms relative to your torso?

15 Do you tend to hit most shots to the left or to the right?

16 Do you stroke putts straight back and straight through or on an arc?

17 Do you consider yourself a "technical" player or a "feel" player?

18 What long-term and short-term goals have you set for your golf game?

As you can see, these eighteen questions cover more than half a dozen general topic areas pertaining to your golf game and lifestyle. Among them are your frequency of play, playing ability, formal training, learning style, economic status, age and physical condition, and personal aspirations. All of these considerations are interrelated, and each can have a significant influence on the type of instructors and the type of swing methods best suited to you. But when it comes to choosing between the two main instructional approaches—error correction and swing development—your frequency of play, your playing ability, and your personal aspirations rank highest on the scale of influence. After examining their influ-

ence in more detail, I'll show you how to cross tabulate these factors to identify your personal golf instruction profile.

▶ Frequency of Play

Let's start with your **frequency of play**, arguably the most important variable in the equation of your golf improvement formula. It is also a variable over which you can exercise a fair amount of personal control. Granted, there may be all manner of extenuating circumstances in your life that limit the number of rounds you can play in any given year. Unless you're a professional golfer, you probably have a nongolf day job. You may have family responsibilities and time constraints. You may live in a cold-climate area where golf courses are closed for several months of the year. Your access to nearby courses may be limited by membership restrictions, financial constraints, even overcrowding.

But at least in theory, your frequency of play is something you can increase if you are determined to do so. Ditto your frequency of practice. You can move from a cold-climate area to a warm-climate area where golf is played year-round, or migrate south in the winter. You can seek out publicly accessible golf courses that have modest green fees and fight the attendant overcrowding, or you can invest your life savings in a membership at a private club where there is relatively little daily play. At the end of the day, it becomes

a matter of individual choice, albeit a potentially costly and disruptive one, inextricably related to your personal aspirations and your desire to improve.

In reality, the vast majority of golfers in America are recreational golfers, not aspiring tournament champions or dedicated professionals. According to a recent participation study by the National Golf Foundation in Jupiter, Florida, 26.4 million people played 564 million rounds of golf in the United States in calendar year 1999. That is an average of 21.3 rounds per person, or slightly less than 2 rounds per person per month. Confirming conventional wisdom, the NGF reports that more than 80 percent of all golfers are male, with an average age of thirty-nine and an average income of $68,000 a year. The average male golfer played about 5 more rounds annually than the average female golfer.

Relatively few golfers, however, play as often as once a week. In fact, the NGF reports that the greatest number of golfers—some 10.6 million, or almost 40 percent of the total golfing population—are "occasional" golfers who play an average of only 3.4 rounds over the span of the entire year. Those people whom the NGF categorizes as "moderate" golfers numbered 7.6 million strong, and played an average of 14.2 rounds, or just a little over once a month. Only 6 million people, roughly 22 percent of the total golfing population, were categorized as "avid" golfers, and they played an average of just 36.6 rounds, roughly 3 rounds per month.

Beginners and golfers at opposite ends of the age spectrum stood out from the rest of their fellow hookers and slicers. There were 3.2 million first-time golfers in 1999, more than twice as many as in 1994. The novices played an average of 10.6 rounds, or three times as often as so-called occasional golfers. The nation's 6.6 million senior golfers, defined as people age fifty and above, played more often than any other demographic group, averaging almost 40 rounds per person annually, but even that was still short of once a week.

Surprisingly enough, the NGF statistics suggest that Tiger Woods's much-heralded role in inspiring young people to take up golf may be overblown or at least rather short-lived. The total number of junior golfers, defined as youth between the ages of twelve and seventeen, actually declined to 2 million in 1999 after rising to a new peak of 2.3 million in 1997, the year Woods won his first Masters. Those junior golfers who stuck with the game played only slightly more often than so-called moderate golfers, averaging just 16.4 rounds annually.

No teaching pro in his or her right mind would suggest that frequency of play is the sole determinant of how well you play at present, or how well you might be able to play in the future. There are plenty of golfers who play every week and even several times a week who don't play very well and probably never will. Playing more golf will by no means guarantee that you will start playing better golf. Indeed, the opposite is often true for a variety of reasons, including poor practice habits and misguided instruction.

But at the same time, it's fair to say that if you are a "moderate" golfer who plays only once a month, or an "occasional" golfer who plays just two or three times a year, your prospects of improving will be relatively limited.

To play better golf, you will probably have to play golf—and practice golf—with greater frequency than you do now. Exactly how much greater frequency depends on the individual. That's where your playing ability comes in.

Playing Ability

Your **playing ability** can be simply defined as your level of golfing prowess at the present time, as measured by your average score. The vast majority of golfers rank pretty low in playing ability in comparison to PGA Tour players. According to the United States Golf Association, only 5 million of America's 26.4 million golfers have certified handicaps. The average handicap for male golfers is 15.7; the average handicap for female golfers is 28.5. But remember that a handicap is really a measure of the potential ability of a player, not an estimate of what the player is likely to shoot on any given day, since it is figured on the best ten of their last twenty rounds. The USGA's handicap researchers report that a player is expected to play to their handicap, or play better, only 25 percent of the time. A player's average score is actually expected to be about three strokes higher than their handicap.

The bottom line is that the average male golfer is hard pressed to break 90 and the average female golfer is hard pressed to break 100 most of the time. And despite the tall tales you may have heard in clubhouse bars, the truth is that relatively few players can break 80 on a consistent basis, much less shoot par or better. According to the USGA, only 20.44 percent of all male golfers, or roughly one in five men, and only 2.09 percent of female golfers, or roughly one in fifty women, have single-digit handicaps that attest to their potential ability to shoot scores in the 70s. Still fewer players have the ability or potential ability to shoot in the 60s. Only a little more than one half of 1 percent of all male golfers, and less than one tenth of 1 percent of all female golfers, have scratch handicaps or better.

That still means, however, there are hordes of expert golfers prowling America's links. While the percentage of players with handicaps of scratch or better may be low relative to the total golfing population, the absolute number is well above 35,000, according to USGA statistics. And even if you're lucky enough to find yourself among the elite group of players who can shoot par consistently, remember that there are still a few thousand golfers who have the ability to break par on a regular basis. Roughly seven hundred of those golfers play full-time or part-time on the PGA Tour, Senior PGA Tour, and the developmental Buy.Com Tour. Another three hundred or so play on the LPGA Tour and the developmental Futures Tour. Hundreds more play on professional mini-tours from coast to coast, or on top-ranked high school and college teams.

So how do you factor your playing ability and your frequency of play when you're mapping out a plan to improve your golf game? Playing ability is a product of nature and nurture, the combination of your innate physical and mental talent and your work ethic. If you're blessed with exceptional talent, you may not have to play and practice as frequently as a less talented golfer to achieve the same level of prowess. The catch is that the better you get, the more you will probably have to play and practice to maintain that higher level of proficiency. There are a few notable exceptions. PGA Tour veteran Bruce Lietzke is envied by his peers for his ability to take off months at a time without losing his form or feel. But virtually all of the reigning stars of the tour, including Tiger Woods, maintain rigorous practice and playing schedules along with physical conditioning regimens.

Most golfers will have to increase their frequency of play and practice if they want to achieve and maintain a higher level of playing ability. Again, the question becomes, How much? The answer depends on where you're starting from and where you want to go. That's where personal aspirations figure in the equation.

Personal Aspirations

Personal aspirations are the golfing goals you set for yourself, and they are by definition unique to each golfer. The premise of this book is that virtually every golfer wants to improve his or her game.

The hope of playing better the next time out is what keeps the vast majority of us coming back for more. Some golfers merely want to play well enough to break 100. Others long to break 90, or shoot consistently in the 80s. Still others dream of breaking 80 or 70. But not everyone aspires to play on the PGA Tour or the LPGA Tour— and more to the point, not everyone can.

Like all of humankind, golfers are limited not only by their dreams. Dreaming and positive thinking are important, to be sure. If you don't believe you can ever break 100, or 90, or 80, you probably never will. If you don't believe that with the proper instruction and proper practice habits you can control that duck hook or cure that slice, you probably never will. But you can dream about being the next Tiger Woods for ten thousand nights and still not come anywhere close to reaching that goal if you don't have the necessary talent and drive, and maybe a good bit of luck, as well.

The point is, you're likely to have the most success in mapping out an effective plan to improve your golf game if you can be realistic about your personal aspirations. The eighteen questions listed at the beginning of this chapter can help guide you in identifying and analyzing the "reality factors" that may pertain to your personal aspirations.

Your age and physical condition are two major reality factors. One of the things that makes golf unique is that it can be played by almost all age groups. Another is that it is a game at which players can excel on the basis of finesse and mental acumen rather than

solely on the basis of strength and power. In fact, the great Sam Snead once wrote a book entitled *Golf Begins at Forty*. But Snead's catchy title applies mostly to recreational golf, not world-class competitive golf. You may still have an outside shot at qualifying for the Senior PGA Tour if you embark on a serious program to improve your golf at age forty, but you'll have almost no chance of keeping up with the young bucks on the PGA Tour, as I found out in my own quest for fame and fortune on the pro golf circuit in 1995 and 1996. And even if you aim for the over-fifty pro circuit, you'd better be in as good physical shape as most of today's Senior PGA Tour stars are.

Time and money are two equally important reality factors. Let's say you're a relatively youthful, physically fit fifteen handicapper who aspires to play scratch golf. Are you really willing to spend the time and money it will likely take to lower your handicap by fifteen strokes? Are you willing to put in the effort required to overhaul your full swing, your short game, and your putting from top to bottom? Or are you really just looking for a quick fix that will cure your slice or reduce your tendency to duck-hook drives under the pressure of a two-dollar bet against the members of your regular Saturday morning foursome?

Here's a quick way to make a reality check on the true level of your aspirations to improve your golf game. It's also the first step in computing a **golf instruction profile scorecard (GIPS)** that will help you identify what type of player you really are and what type of

instruction you really need. Take your current frequency of play and grade it on the following three-point scale:

1   **Monthly:** You play and/or practice golf 12 times per year or less.

2   **Weekly:** You play and/or practice golf between 36 and 52 times per year.

3   **Daily:** You play and/or practice golf an average of at least 4 days per week.

Now let's take the second step toward computing your GIPS by comparing your current frequency of play to the frequency of play typically required to achieve and maintain three selected levels of playing ability as measured by a player's average score:

PLAYING ABILITY	FREQUENCY OF PLAY
1 LOW PROFIENCY (average score 90 or higher)	Monthly
2 MIDDLING PROFICIENCY average score 80–89)	Weekly
3 HIGH PROFICIENCY (average score 79 or lower)	Daily

Chances are that your current frequency of play is nowhere close to the frequency of play required to shoot the kind of scores you wish or hope to shoot. But wishing and hoping alone won't

lower your average score or your handicap. You have to make a choice to improve and a commitment of time to achieve your goal. If, for example, you are a 90s shooter who plays about once a month, you're going to have to start playing and practicing at least once a week if you want to start shooting in the 80s. If your current average score is already in the 80s and you play about once a week, you're going to have to start playing and practicing at least four times a week if you want to start breaking 80 consistently, and considerably more often if you want to shoot scores of par or better.

That is where taking lessons from a first-rate teaching pro can make all the difference. As noted above, playing more golf does not guarantee that you will play better golf. Neither does devoting countless hours on the practice range or the putting green. If you're like most golfers, you need guidance from a qualified instructor in setting short-term, intermediate-term, and long-term goals for improvement, and in devising a specific program to address the strengths and weaknesses of your full swing, your short game, your putting, and your course management skills. Absent such guidance, you may very well end up practicing the wrong things, and further ingraining your bad habits when you go out on the course to play.

But taking golf lessons isn't for everyone. Both one-on-one lessons and golf schools can be very expensive as well as time-consuming. Some of today's leading instructors demand the same rates as doctors and lawyers. Butch Harmon bills lessons at $500

per hour. David Leadbetter gets $5,000 for a minimum four-hour session. Mitchell Spearman insists on a minimum three-hour session for $1,500. Tuition at Jim McLean's three-day golf schools runs over $2,200 per person. One of the reasons these top teaching pros charge such high fees is that they can: their reputations and their track records of improving the games of top tour pros are among the best in the business. Another reason is that many of them prefer to work only with serious students.

With that in mind, it's time to arrive at a decision about the type of instructional approach is best suited to you and your game. Neither your current frequency of play nor your playing ability are in and of themselves the sole determinants. You can still be among the serious golfers who might benefit from taking lessons from a Butch Harmon or a David Leadbetter even if you do not play very often or play very well at the present time.

The decisive test of how serious you are about improving your game is made through assessing your realistic personal aspirations in the context of how often and how well you play now.

▶ Tallying Your GIPS

The golf instruction profile scorecard you've begun computing in the sections above is a formula for measuring your true commitment and need to improve your game based on the three factors

we've been discussing: your frequency of play, your playing ability, and your personal aspirations. The GIPS formula is derived in part from the pioneering studies of individual and small-group behavior done in the 1960s by Harvard University psychologist Robert F. Bales and his associates. Bales found that by ranking members of a group in terms of key behavioral characteristics, it is possible to plot their status relative to each other on a three-dimensional matrix. Using such a matrix also provides a way to categorize individuals into subgroups according to behavioral types.

You've already ranked each of the first two factors on a three-point scale. So let's rank your personal aspirations on a three-point scale:

1   **Low:** You are content with your current level of playing ability.

2   **Middling:** You want to improve your playing ability by 3 to 5 strokes.

3   **High:** You want to improve your playing ability by more than 5 strokes and/or you want to become a high-proficiency player (average score 79 or lower).

All you have to do to tally your GIPS is to write down your three-point scale scores for each of the three factors in the formula: your personal aspirations, your frequency of play, and your playing ability. After you've finished computing your GIPS, use the chart on

Golf Instruction Profile Scorecard (GIPS)

For Players with Middling or High Personal Aspirations

....

FR = frequency of play: (1) monthly, (2) weekly, (3) daily
PL = playing ability: (1) low, (2) middling, (3) high
PA = personal aspirations: (1) low, (2) middling, (3) high

	HUSTLERS	COUNTRY CLUB BUMS	LOCAL LEGENDS
FR	daily (3)	weekly (2)	monthly (1)
PL	high (3)	high (3)	high (3)
PA	middling (2)	middling (2)	middling (2)

	HAPPY HOOKERS AND SLICERS		
FR	monthly (1)	weekly (2)	daily (3)
PL	middling (2)	middling (2)	middling (2)
PA	middling (2)	middling (2)	middling (2)

	HOPEFUL HACKERS	UNHAPPY HACKERS	
FR	monthly (1)	weekly (2)	daily (1)
PL	low (1)	low (1)	low (1)
PA	middling (2)	middling (2)	middling (2)

	DREAMERS	SCHEMERS	STRIVERS
FR	monthly (1)	weekly (2)	daily (1)
PL	low (1)	middling (2)	middling (2)
PA	high (3)	high (3)	high (3)

	STRIVER/DREAMERS	SLACKERS	SLACKER/DREAMERS
FR	daily (3)	monthly (1)	weekly (2)
PL	low (1)	middling (2)	low (1)
PA	high (3)	high (3)	high (3)

	PRO-AMS	SINGLE DIGITS	ONETIME WONDERS
FR	daily (3)	weekly (2)	monthly (1)
PL	high (3)	high (3)	high (3)
PA	high (3)	high(3)	high (3)

page 18 to determine which of the golfer types matches your personal instructional profile.

Right away up to half of you may find that you really don't want to or need to take golf lessons. If you gave your personal aspirations a score of 1 (low), then you are already content with the way you play now, which means there's no point spending time and money on pursuing an instructional program. Continue to play or practice as much or as little as you like, and continue to enjoy what is probably your favorite hole on any course—the nineteenth.

If your playing ability already equals or exceeds a "middling" level of personal aspirations, you are likely to be among one of four instructional profiles who are best advised to make only marginal changes, if any, in their current golfing regimen.

Three of these middling aspiration profiles are familiar fixtures at public, daily fee, and private courses from coast to coast. There's the **Hustler**, who plays several times a week and plays well, but has no aspirations of becoming a pro. There's the **Country Club Bum**, who plays several times a month and plays well, but has no aspirations of becoming a top amateur. And then there's the **Local Legend**, who doesn't play very often but still plays extremely well despite a sometimes mysterious lack of aspiration.

Hustlers, Country Club Bums, and Local Legends can probably shave three to five strokes off their average scores without embarking on a formal instructional program. In most cases, all

they need to do is increase their frequency of play and/or their frequency of practice.

The fourth and most populous of the middling aspiration profiles are the **Happy Hookers and Slicers,** most of whom are actually borderline cases when it comes to prescribing a program of golf instruction. Happy Hookers and Slicers span the entire scale in their frequency of play. Depending on lifestyle, business interests, and other considerations, they may show up at the course or the practice range daily, weekly, or monthly. The one thing all of them have in common is that their middling level of playing ability already matches their middling level of personal aspirations.

As a rule, most Happy Hookers and Slicers are best suited to the most popular approach to golf instruction, which is error correction. They'd be happy to lower their average scores by a few strokes per round, but they're not prepared to devote much time or money to the effort. They much prefer to get quick fixes for their hooks and slices rather than tackle a long-term swing development program that may require extensive changes, retraining, and practice.

Now we come to golfers whose level of personal aspirations exceeds their current level of playing ability. That general category should include the vast majority of people who would read a consumer's guide to golf instruction—i.e., golfers who want to map out an effective plan to improve their games—and it consists of no less than twelve golf instruction profiles.

Depending on who is counting, up to a third of all golfers are either **Hopeful Hackers** or **Unhappy Hackers.** Both types have low playing ability and only middling aspirations. The difference between them is their frequency of play. Hopeful Hackers are primarily beginners who don't play well and don't play very much, but still have optimistic hopes of improving enough to play respectably. Unhappy Hackers go out on the golf course anywhere from three times a month to several times a week; their unhappiness stems from the fact that their hopes of achieving even middling improvement in their games remain unfulfilled no matter how often they play.

Hopeful Hackers and Unhappy Hackers are candidates for either swing development or error correction. The choice depends in part on if they are content to remain with middling aspirations or if they are moved to raise their aspirations. Hopeful Hackers who are just beginning to play golf are often best advised to embark on at least some form of swing development program that provides grounding in the fundamentals, though they don't necessarily have to seek out a Butch Harmon or a David Leadbetter to do the job. Unhappy Hackers typically opt for error correction, but if their Band-Aid fixes have worn off for the umpteenth time, they might be better off in a more thoroughgoing swing development program.

Another six instructional profiles have high personal aspirations that exceed their current level of playing ability. The differences between them are their playing ability and their frequency of

play. On one end of the spectrum are the **Dreamers**, who don't play very well or play very often, but nevertheless dream of dramatic improvement. At the opposite end of the spectrum are the **Strivers**, who have modest playing ability but play several times a week striving to improve.

In between are the hybrid profiles. There are the **Striver/Dreamers**, who have low playing ability but work hard on their games with dreams of playing much better. There are the **Schemers**, who have already have at least middling playing ability but play only a few times a month, believing that they can nevertheless hit upon a scheme to fulfill their high aspirations. There are the **Slackers**, who have middling ability but are too lazy to play frequently enough to fulfill their grandiose aspirations. And there are the **Slacker/Schemers**, who play more than the pure Slackers, but lack the ability of the pure Schemers.

Three main options are available to the various Strivers, Slackers, Dreamers, and Schemers whose personal aspirations exceed their playing ability: (a) they can increase their frequency of play, (b) they can embark on a serious program of golf instruction, or (c) they can do both. The choice ultimately depends on how serious they are about fulfilling their high aspirations.

The last three golf instruction profiles have high aspirations and high playing ability. The difference between them is their frequency of play. Those who play and practice at least several times a week are the

Pro-Ams, tour pros, aspiring tour pros, or top-ranked amateur golfers. Those who play and practice at least several times a month are golfers whose handicaps are in the **Single Digits.** Those who are unable to play more than once a month due to extenuating life circumstances but still shoot low scores are the **Onetime Wonders.**

The majority of these highly proficient golfers have already mapped out their own instructional programs. But even the Pro-Ams can find themselves torn between error correction and swing development approaches. The choice often comes down to how serious they are about fulfilling their high aspirations to take their games to a still higher level. In their cases, given their demonstrated talent, the sky really is the limit. Witness Tiger Woods, who decided to overhaul his swing under the guidance of Butch Harmon after he had already won the 1997 Masters, an endeavor that took more than a year and a half.

The chart on page 25 is designed to help you decide whether you really want to seek error correction, swing development, neither of the two, or a combination of both. It matches GIPS types with their presently preferred instructional approach and the instructional approach recommended for achieving their middling or high personal aspirations.

Getting a Grip on Your GIPS

Once you have done the research necessary to know yourself, your golfing goals, and your preferred and recommended instructional approaches with the help of your GIPS, the next step is to decide which of the various putting, short game, and full swing methods is best suited to you and your game. Most top teaching pros can provide either error correction or swing development instruction. But they often differ dramatically in the putting, short-game, and full-swing methods they advocate. The same goes for the teaching pros you're likely to encounter at your home course or at your local driving range.

No matter which instructional approach you choose, you need to know where your instructors are coming from, which of the major methods they advocate, and the advantages and disadvantages of each. Otherwise, you are likely to find yourself bouncing from one pro to another, perpetually trapped in states of confusion and frustration as you are inundated with conflicting advice and diametrically opposite swing thoughts. No one knows that better than I do after taking lessons from twenty-one different teaching pros in twenty-four months. Instead of suffering the pain and confusion of running a similar instructional gauntlet, you can simply read this book.

Preferred and Recommended
Instructional Approaches

According to Golf Instruction Profile Scorecard (GIPS)

· · · · · · · · · · · · · · · · ·

Pr = instructional approach preferred by golfer
Re = instructional approach recommended for golfer

	HUSTLERS	COUNTRY CLUB BUMS	LOCAL LEGENDS
Pr	none	none	none
Re	none	none	none

	HAPPY HOOKERS AND SLICERS
Pr	error correction/none
Re	error correction/none

	HOPEFUL HACKERS		UNHAPPY HACKERS
Pr	error correction		error correction
Re	swing development		swing development

	DREAMERS	SCHEMERS	STRIVERS
Pr	error correction	error correction	swing development
Re	swing development	error correction	swing development

	STRIVER/DREAMERS	SLACKERS	SLACKER/DREAMERS
Pr	swing development	none	none
Re	swing development	error correction	error correction

	PRO-AMS	SINGLE DIGITS	ONETIME WONDERS
Pr	both approaches	error correction	error correction
Re	both approaches	swing development	error correction

SUMMARY: *Making a Plan to Improve Your Game*

Regardless of whether you're a hooker or a slicer, the key to mapping out an effective learning program is to know yourself. The list of "Eighteen Questions to Ask Yourself Before Taking a Lesson" can help in the self-assessment process.

▶ FREQUENCY OF PLAY, PLAYING ABILITY, AND PERSONAL ASPIRATIONS

Most golfers will have to increase their frequency of play (and practice) if they want to play better golf than they do now. How much you will have to increase your frequency of play depends on current playing ability and your personal aspirations. You will likely have the most success and gain the most enjoyment out of the learning process if you can be realistic about your personal aspirations.

▶ ERROR CORRECTION VS. SWING DEVELOPMENT

There are two main approaches to instruction: error correction and swing development. Error correction focuses on fixing a specific swing flaw or problem right away; it is by definition primarily a short-term or "Band-Aid" solution. Swing development focuses on building or overhauling your golf game from top to bottom; it is long-term in nature and can require considerable time, effort, and money.

▶Consult Your Golf Instruction Profile Scorecard (GIPS)

Your golf instruction profile scorecard (GIPS) is a formula for measuring your true commitment and need to improve your game based on your frequency of play, your playing ability, and your personal aspirations. Consult the chart on page 18 to determine which of the GIPS types best describes you. Consult the chart on page 25 to determine whether error correction or swing development is recommended for your GIPS type.

2 HOLE OUT FIRST:
Picking Your Own Path to Great Putting

If golf is the name of the game, the object of the game is to get the ball into the hole in the fewest strokes possible. The rules of golf permit every player to carry a maximum of fourteen clubs as the means to that end. If you're like me and millions of other hookers and slicers, you've undoubtedly had days when none of the damn sticks in your bag seems capable of getting the ball anywhere near the hole, much less all the way into it. That can be especially true of the club expressly designed for the singular purpose of holing out—your putter.

Great golfers and great golf instructors have long debated which of the fourteen clubs you're allowed to carry is the single most important. Ben Hogan insisted that three clubs deserved to be ranked as foremost in the following order: the driver, the putter, and the wedge. Harvey Penick took issue with Hogan, insisting that the proper ordering was the putter, the driver, and the wedge.

"Psychologically, the driver is very important," Penick noted in his *Little Red Book*. "If you hit your tee ball well, it fills you with confidence. . . . But nothing is more important psychologically than knocking putts into the hole. Sinking putts makes your confidence soar, and it devastates your opponent."

The overriding importance of the putter is affirmed by the standards the United States Golf Association uses to establish par. When USGA course raters determine that a particular hole is a par three, they are saying that under normal conditions they expect an expert player to be able to reach the green in one stroke, and hole out in two more strokes. On a par four, they expect an expert player to be able to reach the green in two strokes, and hole out in two more. On a par five, they expect an expert player to be able to reach the green in three strokes, and hole out in two more.

No wonder so many great golfers and great golf instructors, with the notable exceptions of Hogan and a few others, maintain that putting is at least half the game. Just do the math. On a typical par seventy-two course, an expert player is expected to play an average of thirty-six strokes from tee to green, and an average of thirty-six strokes on the green. You can't get more half-and-half than that.

Of course, few golfers expect to take two putts on each hole, and better players are extremely dissatisfied if they do. Dave Pelz, a leading short-game instructor who once worked at the National Aeronautics and Space Administration (NASA), calculates that put-

ting actually represents approximately 43 percent of all shots played by all golfers regardless of ability in any given round. According to his research, a 70 shooter averages thirty putts per round, an 85 shooter averages thirty-five putts per round, and a 95 shooter averages thirty-eight putts per round.

Even so, Pelz declares in his seminal 1989 book, *Putt Like the Pros*, "In reality, putting is more than half the game!" The reasons are both logistical and psychological. Unless you happen to hit your ball into the cup from the fairway or from somewhere off the green, the one club you're guaranteed to use on every hole is your putter. What's more, your putting stroke can profoundly affect the way you play the rest of your golf shots. You will likely be able to swing more freely (and be more accurate) with your woods and irons if you know you've got a good chance of nailing those fifteen- and twenty-foot putts. Conversely, if you lack confidence in your putting, you will likely be tempted to try to guide or steer your approach shots to within "gimmie" distance, which is more often than not a formula for disaster.

Like the full swing, putting has evolved with changes in technology, as well as with changes in golf course design and maintenance. In the early days of the game, greens were much lumpier and slower than they are today because of the relatively primitive state of agronomy. Putters were made almost entirely of wood with shafts that attached to the heel of the hitting face, and they were also

fairly high-lofted (often 10 degrees or more) in order to get the ball rolling over the bumps. As course maintenance improved, greens became smoother and faster. Now putters are less lofted (most are between 2 degrees and 8 degrees), and they are made of all sorts of metals and composite materials in both heel-shafted and center-shafted models with a wide variety of lengths and head shapes.

Perhaps the only thing that has remained constant about putting since the birth of the royal and ancient game is that "proper" putting technique has always been regarded as a highly idiosyncratic affair. While many great golfers and great golf instructors have sought or advocated a certain conformity in ball-striking styles, putting styles have been permitted an unusually wide berth. "The putting stroke is probably the game's most individualistic area," Tiger Woods's coach, Butch Harmon, notes in his instructional manual *The Four Cornerstones of Winning Golf:* "There are a remarkable number of great putters whose styles are different from one another."

Like great ball strikers, great putters are sometimes divided into two main types—hookers and slicers. But such a categorization is not really accurate. As many top instructors and students of the game point out, it is almost impossible to curve a putt to the left or to the right in the same way that you can hook or slice a shot with an iron or a driver. The reasons have to do with friction and aerodynamics. To put it most simply, a ball struck with a putter generally remains snug to the grass (notwithstanding an initial skid phase

and various random hops or bounces), and the friction between grass and ball tends to reduce the kind of sidespin that can occur when a ball is lofted into the air.

Be that as it may, both great and not-so-great putters seem to roll the ball with a directional bias that is either a "pull" to the left or a "push" to the right. The late South African star Bobby Locke, who won four British Opens between 1949 and 1957, and two-time Masters champion Ben Crenshaw have been branded hookers, if only because they created the appearance of hooking their putts by opening and closing the faces of their putters during their strokes. In his heyday, Billy Casper managed remarkably true rolls with his wristy "rapping" stroke. George Archer has been acclaimed as a straight putter with a near-perfect pendulum stroke. But the vast majority of putters appear to cut, shove, or block their putts to the right. Jack Nicklaus is by far the most successful "shove" putter of all time. Lee Trevino is a phenomenal "blocker." Chi Chi Rodriguez is still one of the world's deadliest "cutters."

In recent years, Pelz and others have endeavored literally to straighten out the putting strokes of their disciples, and to transform putting into a science with the application of insights derived from physics, biomechanics, and ophthalmology. But despite the advent of high-tech instructional aids ranging from laser-beam-aiming devices to a Pelz-designed putting robot dubbed "Perfy," putting is still regarded as a true art. That will likely continue to be

the case for several reasons. Under actual playing conditions out on a course, a golfer must rely on feel for distances, slopes, and breaks in addition to a consistent stroke in order to get the ball into the hole. And as most golfers can attest, the closer you get to the hole, the more psychology and emotion enter the picture.

So what is the best way for a beginner to learn to putt and the best way for an experienced player to learn to putt better?

Like the art of putting itself, the answer depends on the individual. There is no such thing as the one perfect putting stroke or the one perfect putting method that suits all golfers. In fact, at least three major types of putting strokes are currently in use on the PGA Tour, with countless permutations and combinations of each. If you ask twenty top-ranked teaching pros to describe the most desirable putting technique in specific detail, you're likely to get half a dozen different answers.

While there may be no one right way to putt, you can inadvertently make many wrong turns on the road to improving your putting. One of the most treacherous pitfalls is confusing and/or trying to commingle the principles of one putting method with the principles of another putting method. A second commonly encountered mistake is switching back and forth between putters and putting methods for no apparent rhyme or reason other than frustration or superstition. But both beginners and experienced golfers can avoid these and other missteps by following a two-step approach to better putting.

The first step in leaning how to improve your putting stroke is to evaluate the main options available. The next steps are to pick your path and putting method, pick your putter, pick your instructor, and then stick with them.

Three Paths to Perfect Putting

For our purposes, **path** can be defined as the direction along which your putter head travels relative to your intended aim line. Observing the path made by the putter head is the most visible way to tell the difference between various types of putting strokes and putting methods. (Given that you will be unable to observe your own putting stroke without moving your head and thereby altering the path, ask a teaching pro or a friend to help you identify it.) Path is also the aspect of putting that most golfers and most golf instructors tend to work on the most—though, as we shall see, it is neither the only nor the most important aspect.

Most putting paths belong to one of three configurative categories: lines, semicircles, and loops. Certain advocates of one path will tell you that the other paths are "wrong." But such a statement is not fair or accurate. Given that all three of these paths have been successfully employed by leading PGA Tour pros, it is more objective and accurate to say that each has its advantages and disadvantages. Some paths may be judged simpler and more straightforward

than others. Some may require more precise timing and higher maintenance (i.e., more practice) than others. And some may simply feel more comfortable than others, an important consideration in light of the highly personal nature of putting.

The **line path** is currently enjoying great popularity among tour pros and teaching pros, thanks in part to Pelz, whose statistics-laden books and magazine articles suggest that it is the most efficient path. A line is, after all, the shortest and straightest path on which to travel between two points. What's more, moving your putter straight back and straight through on a line path keeps the putter head square to and on top of your intended aim line throughout the stroke. Advocates claim that that means a line path does not require the same kind of precise timing to square the putter head at impact that may be required in certain strokes that make a semicircular path or a looping path.

The line path is commonly associated with the **pure pendulum stroke.** As the term implies, a pure pendulum stroke resembles the motion of a pendulum, like that found on a grandfather clock. One of the claimed advantages of the pure pendulum putting stroke is that it does not involve hand or wrist action. Rather, a pure pendulum stroke is typically made by rocking the shoulders up and down in a motion often compared to that used when rocking a baby. A pure pendulum stroke can be made using a short-shafted putter with a conventional overlapping grip, a reverse overlapping grip, a

"Line Path" (Pure Pendulum Stroke)

right hand "claw" grip, or a cross-handed (left hand low) grip, as well as with long-shafted and intermediate-length putters gripped in split-handed fashion. Among the PGA Tour stars using a pure pendulum stroke or slightly modified form of the pure pendulum stroke are Peter Jacobsen, former Masters and PGA champion Vijay Singh, and two-time U.S. Open champion Lee Janzen.

Ironically, the rocking action of the pure pendulum stroke is often cited as one of its major drawbacks. Although the shaft of the putter does not deviate from the intended aim line of a putt, the putter head does move up and then down and then up again from backswing to follow-through. Critics point out that in the process, the putter face closes and opens relative to a vertically planed arc, thereby requiring precise timing to square the face at the trough of the arc when making impact with the ball. They claim that the up-

"Semicircle Path" (Arc Stroke)

down-up motion of the pure pendulum stroke "feels unnatural," especially under the heat of competition.

The pure pendulum motion also requires you to establish a fairly precise ball position on every stroke. If your ball position changes either forward or backward, you're likely to strike the ball too much on the upswing or too much on the downswing. Likewise, your distance from the ball is critical. Ideally, you want to keep your eyes directly over the target line in order to keep your stroke on line as well. You can sometimes get away with having your eyes slightly inside the line, but you're likely to push your putts to the right if your eyes get too far inside the line. If your eyes are outside the target line, you're likely to pull your putts to the left.

One further note: Just because your putter moves in a line path, that does not necessarily mean you are using a pure pendulum

stroke in the classic or strictest sense. You can also putt on line paths that are at cross-angles to your stance line and/or your intended aim line. Golfers who "shove" or "block" their putts to the right à la Jack Nicklaus or Lee Trevino have fairly straight line paths that move "inside-out," while golfers who "cut" their putts à la Chi Chi Rodriguez have fairly straight line paths that move "outside-in."

The **semicircle** path is probably the oldest and most traditional putting path. It moves from square at address to "inside" on the backswing, back to square at impact, and then to the "inside" on the through swing. In contrast to the line path, the semicircle path made by the putter is a kind of miniature version of the path made by longer clubs on chips and full swings. That is cited as one of its major advantages. To put it in simplest terms, if you putt in a semicircle path, you can use the same basic motion on the green that you use from tee to green.

The semicircle path is commonly associated with the **arc putting stroke,** also known as the "swinging gate." It is typically made with a conventional-length putter using an overlapping or reverse overlapping grip. Among the PGA Tour stars who have demonstrated the merits of the arc stroke are Ben Crenshaw, who is widely acclaimed to be one of the greatest putters of all time, and Tiger Woods, who is rapidly gaining a reputation as *the* greatest putter of all time. The arc stroke is often described as an open-to-closed stroke because the putter head opens relative to the target line on

the backswing and closes relative to the target line on the through swing. But advocates of the arc stroke like Woods's coach, Butch Harmon, contend the open-to-closed moniker is a misnomer. In a perfectly executed arc stroke, they say, the goal is to keep the putter head square to the path—not the target line—throughout the stroke.

"If the putter head remains square to the path throughout the entire stroke, this means it will automatically be square to the target line at impact," Harmon declares in *Four Cornerstones of Winning Golf.* "You should not try to keep the putter face pointed directly at the target throughout the entire stroke, because to do so you would have to manipulate the putter face with your hands and forearms in an unnatural way."

In answer to Harmon, critics insist that the arc stroke is a high-maintenance method that's not nearly as "natural" as he suggests. Like the pure pendulum stroke, the arc stroke can be powered primarily by rocking the triangle formed by the shoulders, arms, and hands in what is typically described as a "pendulum-like" or "pendulum-style" motion. But many golfers who use the arc stroke seem to employ at least some degree of hand, wrist, or forearm rotation, and occasionally some body action, to help them square the putter head at impact with the ball.

The arc stroke also requires even more exacting ball position than the pure pendulum stroke. If the ball is too far back, you're likely to push your putts to the right. If the ball is too far forward,

"Loop Path" (Loop Stroke)

you're likely to pull your putts to the left. As a rule, golfers who favor the arc stroke use a long flowing motion. That places a high premium on maintaining a smooth pace throughout the stroke. Arc putters are often great lag putters. On the other hand, they often encounter problems on short putts, where they can be prone to decelerate or overaccelerate through impact.

The **loop path** is undoubtedly the least common and most fragile of the three main path types. As the term implies, the putter head actually travels in a kind of figure eight pattern on the backswing. Sometimes the movement is in a counterclockwise direction, but more often than not it is in a clockwise direction. Many high-handicap amateurs loop their putters involuntarily or inadvertently as a result of moving their heads, moving their bodies, and/or using too much hand or wrist action on the backswing. Top

golf instructors never recommend putting with a loop path because of its obvious and inherent inconsistencies. A loop path putter needs exceptional timing and a deft ability to manipulate his hands, wrists, and forearms to get the putter back on his intended aim line and to square the putter head at impact.

As if to attest that there is always an exception that proves the rule, the loop path has been used successfully on the PGA Tour. Since turning pro in 1988, loop path putter Billy Mayfair has won over $6 million in prize money. Among his notable accomplishments are winning the 1995 Tour Championship and beating Tiger Woods in a playoff to win the 1998 Nissan Open. Interestingly enough, Mayfair makes an almost picture-perfect line path with his practice strokes, and claims that he is unaware of making a loop with his actual putting stroke despite the incontrovertible evidence of a figure eight provided by the television cameras broadcasting his play on the greens.

That brings us to an important point about putting in general and putting paths in particular—path is only the third most influential factor in a putting stroke. Some of the most compelling evidence comes from the anecdotal information and experience of top players and top teaching pros over several decades. But Pelz also offers persuasive, if independently unconfirmed, statistical support for this point. He reports that his proprietary studies show that only 20 percent of errors in the path of a putting stroke are actually transmitted to the line on which the ball rolls.

The relatively modest influence of path errors underscores the even greater influence of two other factors in putting—face angle and impact point. The reason why Billy Mayfair can be successful with his otherwise ungainly loop path is that he still manages to stroke his putts with the proper face angle at the proper impact point on his putter face.

Face Angle and Impact Point

Face angle can be defined as the direction in which the putter face is looking at impact relative to the intended target line. By definition, face angle errors are a matter of degree, but generally speaking, the face of your putter can either be square, open, or closed to your intended target line at the moment of impact with the ball. Obviously, the ideal face angle is square to the target line. Why? Because as most great putters and putting gurus point out, the ball will start rolling in the direction the face of your putter is pointing, not along the path on which your putter is moving.

The influence of face angle errors is many times greater than the influence of path errors in a putting stroke. Exactly how much greater is open to debate, though the consensus on this point is wide enough to make precise quantification almost moot. Here again, the most compelling evidence comes from anecdotal and experiential information gathered by top players and top teaching pros over sev-

Face Angle: Square

Face Angle: Open

Face Angle: Closed

eral decades. But Pelz has also weighed in with statistics based on his proprietary studies. He reports that if the face of your putter head is not square to the target line at impact, an estimated 90 percent of the error will be transmitted to your ball line.

The problem in correcting face angle errors is that they are almost impossible to see with the naked eye. That's why many leading instructors now videotape putting strokes just as they videotape full swings; some also use laser aiming devices in their putting classes. Many face angle errors originate with a faulty setup and/or an incorrect alignment at address. Flaws in your setup and alignment often result from conscious or unconscious compensations made after witnessing putts miss consistently to the left or to the right due to path errors. The most common error among high- and middle-handicap golfers is a stroke path that moves left and a face angle that points right, producing putts that consistently miss to the right of the intended target line.

Impact point can be defined as the point at which your putter face makes contact with the ball. There are three basic possibilities. You can hit the ball on or toward the heel of the putter, in which case the toe will kick forward and the ball will roll to the left of your aim line. You can hit the ball on or toward the toe of the putter, in which case the heel will kick forward and the ball will roll to the right of your aim line. Or you can hit the ball on the "sweet spot" of the putter, in which case the ball will roll straight down your aim line, provided the putter face angle is also square.

Impact Point: Center

Impact Point: Heel

Impact Point: Toe

The sweet spot, which is also known as the center of percussion, is the point on the face where the putter can strike the ball solidly without producing unwanted movement at the heel or the toe. It is important to note that, depending on the design and weighting characteristics of your putter, the sweet spot may or may not be in the center of the face equidistant from the heel and the toe. One easy way to find the sweet spot is by suspending your putter above the ground with one hand and then tapping the putter face with the tip of a ballpoint pen until you hit upon the spot where impact with the ballpoint does not cause either the heel or the toe to kick backward.

Finding the sweet spot on your putter is essential to improving your putting, regardless of which type of stroke you favor, because impact point is probably the most influential factor in determining the outcome of a putt. There is wide consensus on this point among top players and top teachers based on anecdotal and experiential information. But for once, even Pelz stops short of offering a firm statistic. As he notes in *Putt Like the Pros,* "the degree of error [caused by faulty impact] depends on how far you stroke the ball away from the putter's center of percussion, the weight distribution of the putter being used, and the putter's shaft axis." Pelz nevertheless estimates that 95 percent of the impact error will be transmitted to your ball line.

The reasons for this high influence of impact point are twofold. As already noted, hitting the ball toward the heel or toward

the toe will affect the direction of your putt, starting it either to the left or to the right. But hitting the ball off the center of the putter face also reduces the speed at which your putts will roll, which means that the ball will likely break more. A ball hit solidly on the sweet spot will roll faster and hold its line better.

To sum up, a wide range of putting paths have been used successfully by great golfers, including the line path, the semicircle path, and the loop path, which are respectively associated with the pendulum stroke, the arc stroke, and the figure eight stroke. Each of these methods has advantages and disadvantages in terms of degree of difficulty, required maintenance, and overall comfort and feel. In weighing the options, you should consider which path will most consistently enable you to strike the ball on the sweet spot of your putter with a square face angle.

Picking Your Putter

Once you have picked your path and putting method, it's time to pick a putter that goes with them. In many ways, picking a putter is like picking a spouse. No one but you can really say whom you should marry. As noted above, putting is a highly personal affair, and all sorts of highly personal considerations figure into picking a putter. Cosmetic and visual appeal rank high on the list. So do overall weight, length, handling, and feel. But you can usually be sure from

the outset that certain potential spouses are simply not your type. The same goes for certain putters relative to your chosen stroke.

The style and shape of your putter head is mainly a cosmetic consideration. The majority of golfers and most tour pros prefer some form of blade putter. But several Senior PGA Tour stars and many veteran amateurs still prefer to putt with "old-fashioned" mallet heads. There can be a utilitarian issue here for a rare few. PGA Tour star Notah Begay III, who routinely putts either right- or left-handed depending on the direction in which his putts break, requires a specially designed Bulls Eye blade. (Begay adopted his ambidextrous putting style at Stanford after reading a study that showed that right-handers are more proficient at making left-breaking putts, and left-handers are more proficient at making right-breaking putts. He concedes, however, that he still feels awkward putting left-handed.) Other advocates of blade putters claim they like to have the option of switching sides of the ball to execute trouble shots. But in most cases, the choice between mallet and blade boils down to which of the two most appeals to your eye.

By contrast, the style and shape of your putter shaft should be chosen on the basis of the type of putting stroke you use. Where choosing putter heads is a cosmetic issue, choosing putter shafts is a utilitarian issue. The key considerations here are the length of the shaft, the point at which the shaft attaches to the putter head, and the amount of offset or lack thereof in the shaft.

Pure-pendulum-stroke putters. Golfers who putt on a line path with a pure pendulum stroke have three recommended shaft lengths from which to choose: short, intermediate, and long. Note that the so-called standard-length shaft is not included in this list. The standard-length putter shaft produced by most putter manufactures measures 36 inches. As many top instructors typically warn their students, this is too long for most golfers who putt with conventional overlapping, reverse overlapping, right hand "claw," or cross-handed ("left hand low") grips.

You can determine the proper length for a short-shaft putter simply by assuming your posture, letting your arms hang naturally from your shoulders, and then joining your hands. Most golfers, including those well over six feet tall, will find that their hands join somewhere between 33 inches and 27 inches above the base of the putter shaft. Either choke down to that point or, better yet, install a shaft with the length that fits you (simply trimming the shaft will change the flex and weight balance).

Golfers who prefer the long putter favored by PGA Tour players Scott McCarron and Rocco Mediate and several Senior PGA Tour players need to consider two factors in determining the proper shaft length: their overall height and their hinge point. If you hinge the putter at your chest, the shaft should reach to the top of your sternum. If you hinge the shaft at your chin, the top of the shaft should reach to your Adam's apple.

Long Putter

Center-Shafted Putter

It is worth noting in passing that the advent of the long putter has resurrected the idea broached decades ago by three-time British Open champion Henry Cotton of carrying two flat sticks—in this case, a long putter and a short putter. Many of those who have switched from the short putter claim that the long putter is superior on flat putts within twenty feet of the hole but lacks the "feel" of the short putter on lengthy, undulating putts. Interestingly enough, golfers who have switched from a conventional grip to a cross-handed, or left-hand-low, grip say that the cross-handed grip is better on short putts, while the conventional grip is better on long putts.

Golfers who prefer the intermediate shaft that has been used by PGA Tour pros Vijay Singh and Paul Azinger also need to consider their overall height in determining the proper length. Rather than hinging the putter at your sternum or your chin, you hinge the intermediate-shaft putter at your belly button. With a little experimentation, you can find a length that allows you to bend over just enough to place the butt end of the shaft in your hinge point while still keeping your eyes on top of (as opposed to inside or beyond) your aim line.

Regardless of which length you choose, golfers who decide to putt with a pure pendulum stroke will be best served by the so-called center-shafted putter, whose shaft is attached either at the center of the putter head or between the heel and the center. A center-shafted putter allows you to keep your hands directly below your shoulders and your eyes

directly on top of your aim line. The amount of offset you choose is basically a matter of visual appeal and feel. Since all putters have at least a few degrees of forward lean, your hands will automatically be slightly ahead of the ball at address if you square the face properly. The more offset, the more ahead of the ball your hands will be at address.

Arc putters. Golfers who prefer to putt in a semicircular path with an arc stroke will have fewer putter options than those who prefer the pendulum stroke. Neither long-shafted nor intermediate-shafted putters are suitable to an arc stroke because they require hinge points at the stomach, chest, or chin, and thus do not easily permit you to swing on a semicircular path without excessive body action.

That leaves arc strokers to choose between various types of putters with short shafts. Many prefer so-called heel-shafted putters whose shafts attach at or toward the heel rather than at the center. Crenshaw uses a classic Wilson 8802 model, also known as "Little Ben," whose shaft attaches right on the heel with a small amount of offset that he effectively increases by making a slight forward press with his hands to initiate his stroke. Woods, however, uses a center-shafted Titleist Scotty Cameron putter with a moderate amount of offset.

Regardless of which type of putter you choose, most top teaching pros will tell you to stick with it rather than switching back and forth between different models. As with any other rule, there are some notable exceptions. Senior PGA Tour star Dave Stockton will generally use a low-lofted putter if he happens to be playing on bent-grass

Heel-Shafted Putter

Gravity Golf Putter

HOW TO LEARN GOLF

greens that are smooth and fast. If the greens are lumpier Bermuda grass, he generally uses a higher-lofted putter to get the ball rolling on top of the grain. But most amateur golfers who keep switching putters consciously or unconsciously wind up switching paths and putting methods, and as a result never groove a consistent stroke.

Holing Out First

As you've probably noticed, the names of two contemporary golf instructors—Dave Pelz and Butch Harmon—keep coming up in our discussion of putting methods. There are two reasons. First, Pelz and Harmon are among the top-ranked teaching pros in the business, according to the *Golf Digest* poll of their peers. Secondly, Pelz and Harmon represent two polar opposites when it comes to choosing putting methods and putting instruction. Pelz is the leading advocate of the pendulum stroke; Harmon is the leading advocate of the arc stroke.

The majority of first-rate putting instructors belong to either the Pelz or the Harmon camp, though there are still significant differences in approach from one individual to the next. Darrell Kestner, who is both a top-one-hundred teaching pro and an accomplished tournament player, puts special emphasis on the importance of face angle and impact point in teaching the pure pendulum stroke. Michael Hebron departs from Pelz in encouraging his students to use a forward hand position to "compress" the ball at

impact. (Pelz claims that a putting stroke does not truly compress the ball.) And some iconoclasts straddle the main methodologies. David Lee, the inventor of the Gravity Golf system, teaches a highly modified version of the arc stroke using a specially designed putter with an intermediate-length shaft.

The key considerations in seeking and finding the best golf instruction and in picking the teaching pro who is right for you will be covered in detail in chapter 6. You can get a head start on determining which instructors favor your chosen putting method by consulting the summary on pages 60–61. In the meantime, it is interesting to note that despite the obvious differences between the Pelz camp and the Harmon camp, there are at least three points on which they agree:

1 **Eliminate body action and limit wrist action.** Both pure-pendulum putters and arc putters should eliminate body action in their strokes, and reduce or eliminate excessive hand and wrist action. This dictum is based in part on the fact that modern agronomy has made today's putting surfaces much smoother and faster than the greens of old, thereby eliminating the need for the wristy "raps" and handsy "hits" common to the old-fashioned putting methods once favored by the likes of Billy Casper and Arnold Palmer. With rare exceptions like David Lee, most top teaching pros insist that any body movement during a putting stroke will increase the likelihood of path, face angle, and impact point errors.

2 Shoulders for power, hands for feel. Both pure-pendulum putters and arc putters should rely primarily on the rocking of their shoulders to power their strokes, and rely on their hands and arms almost exclusively to promote feel. This dictum is based in part on the fact that the "big muscles" of the shoulders appear to operate more consistently under pressure than the "small muscles" of the wrists and hands. Be that as it may, some top-ranked teaching pros like Jim Flick, a proponent of the small-muscle full swing, still maintain that the hands and arms are the best sources of feel in the putting stroke, and even Harmon recommends maintaining a little "play" in the wrists to enhance feel. Jack Nicklaus uses a piston-like action of his right forearm to power his stroke.

3 Stick with your pick. Both pendulum putters and arc putters should stick with their chosen method and an instructor who can teach it effectively. You can't learn an arc stroke from a teacher who exclusively advocates the pendulum stroke or vice versa. And you can't fix problems that may arise in a pendulum stroke by resorting to arc stroke methods, or vice versa. While it sometimes makes sense to try a different putting method if your original method is not working, constantly switching back and forth between putting methods and putting instructors will only make you a jack of all trades and a master of none. Here again, I speak from painful but enlightening experience. In the course of researching this book, I've

jacked putts with almost every type of putter and putting method under the sun, and I remain light years away from playing in a Masters or putting like one.

SUMMARY: *Top Teaching Pros and Their Putting Methods*

Although a wide variety of putting methods have been used by great players, the two most popular are the arc stroke and the pure pendulum stroke. In weighing the options, you should consider which path will most consistently enable you to strike the ball on the "sweet spot" of your putter with a square face angle at impact.

▶ PURE PENDULUM STROKE

The pure pendulum stroke follows a line path and the up-down-up arc of a pendulum like that on a grandfather clock. It is usually powered by rocking the shoulders with no hand or wrist action. Advocates claim it is the simplest, most efficient method because the putter face remains square to target line throughout stroke. Critics contend the pure pendulum stroke requires unnatural movement of shoulders and arms, and feels awkward under pressure. Recommended for use with center-shafted putters with conventional, intermediate, or long shafts. Outstanding pure-pendulum-stroke putters include George Archer and Lee Janzen.

Jim Flick, Hank Haney, Michael Hebron, Darrell Kestner,
Dave Pelz

▶ ARC STROKE

Also described as "swinging gate," the arc stroke is the oldest and
most traditional putting method. It follows a semicircular path and is
powered by a "pendulum-like" rocking of the shoulders. The putter
face opens and closes relative to the target line but remains square to
the path of stroke. Advocates claim the arc stroke is the most natural
stroke because it resembles a miniature version of full swing. Critics
contend it puts too much burden on timing and requires manipulation of hands and arms. Recommended for use with heel-shafted
putters of conventional length or specially designed intermediate-
length arc putters. Outstanding arc-stroke putters include Ben Crenshaw and Tiger Woods.

**Jimmy Ballard, Chuck Cook, Butch Harmon, David Leadbetter,
David Lee, Jim McLean, Rick Smith, Bob Toski**

3 FIND YOUR SWING:
Picking Your Own
"Perfect" Motion

Ask just about any golfer what he wants more than anything else in the world, and he will probably reply with the following four words: "A perfect golf swing." The search for the perfect swing has been going on since the royal and ancient game began. It is common to golfers at every level of ability from rank novices to veteran PGA Tour players. It is what inspires us to seek out the best instructors, to pose in front of mirrors and video cameras, to perform all sorts of body-contorting and mind-bending drills, and to spend countless hours bashing balls on the practice range.

Take it from me, the search for the perfect golf swing is an existential exercise in futility that makes the mythological Sisyphus's efforts to roll his rock to the top of the mountain seem like a piece of cake. I haven't been able to find it with the help of twenty-one top-ranked teaching pros, and I know now that I still wouldn't find it if I kept taking lessons from here to eternity. I've also come to

realize that even if I could find the perfect golf swing, it would not make all my golfing dreams come true.

"Most golfers believe that if they can build a perfect golf swing, they can play perfect golf, but that's folly," top-ten teaching pro Jim McLean declares in his book *Golf School*. "Nobody has ever built a perfect golf swing. And even if you could, you'd still have to master three other areas of the game, the short game, the course management game, and the mental/emotional game."

Of course, as the legendary Byron Nelson once observed of his star pupil Tom Watson, winner of eight major championships, that does not mean the perfectionists among us will ever stop trying. "Tom will never be satisfied with his swing," Nelson allowed. "Even if he got to the point where he was hitting every shot just right, he would still find something he wanted to change." Curtis Strange, the first player to win back-to-back U.S Opens since Ben Hogan, expressed similar sentiments in a speech at the PGA of America's 2000 Teaching and Coaching Summit. "I never liked my golf swing, in all honesty, so I kept messing with it," Strange admitted. "I knew how to hit it straight, but I wanted to hit it higher and a little bit farther."

While Watson has continued his tournament-winning ways on the Senior PGA Tour, Strange, who is currently a television golf commentator, can be counted among those unfortunate souls whose search for the perfect swing apparently hastened the demise

of their once glorious golfing careers. Another well-known name on that list is Ian Baker-Finch. After winning the 1992 British Open with a long, upright swing, Baker-Finch tried to make his swing flatter and more rounded in hopes of improving his accuracy; he has since joined Strange in the television commentator's booth. Seve Ballesteros abandoned the powerful if sometimes erratic motion that won him five major championships between the ages of twenty-two and thirty-one and tried to develop a more angular swing; he has failed to contend in a major in over a decade.

What are the lessons you should learn from these cautionary examples if you are among the millions of hookers and slicers who want to improve their golf swings?

The first lesson is that there is really no such thing as the perfect swing, and the search for one can be disastrous as well as eternally frustrating. The closest approximation to a perfect swing is the so-called ModelPro swing. Developed from a statistically refined composite of films of more than one hundred top players, the ModelPro swing has recently been used for comparative analysis on television broadcasts of PGA Tour tournaments. But as will be further detailed below, the ModelPro itself is actually a computerized graphic simulation, not a real human being.

The second and more important lesson is that you can still find a swing that is "perfect" for you and your own golfing goals, just as

the above-mentioned great players did early in their careers, even if it does not match the ideal pictured on some computer simulation, videotape, or instructional manual.

If you choose to view the evolution of swing mechanics from a historical perspective, you can find at least three major types of swings currently in use by leading players on the PGA Tour and the Senior PGA Tour. They can be categorized in order of appearance as the **small-muscle swing**, which relies primarily on the small muscles of the hands, wrists, forearms, and knees; the **big-muscle swing**, which relies primarily on the big muscles of the torso; and the **mixed-muscle swing**, which combines small-muscle and big-muscle power sources.

If you choose to view golf swings from a biomechanical perspective, you can also find three distinct types of swings currently in use on the professional tours. They can be categorized according to power source as the **leverage swing**, used by players of average build and flexibility; the **arc swing**, used by long-armed and exceptionally flexible players; and the **width swing**, used by short-armed, muscular players.

While there may be no such thing as the one perfect swing, each of these swing methods can be deemed "perfect" on its own terms. Each of them has been used by top players. Each of them can claim advocates among the top teaching pros. Each of them has innumerable permutations and combinations, hybrids and subtypes. Each of them has its advantages and disadvantages when

judged on the basis of degree of difficulty, required maintenance, power, accuracy, and consistency.

So how do you go about choosing the swing method that is "perfect" for you?

One of the key considerations in choosing between swing methods is whether you are a hooker or a slicer. For reasons that will be explained in detail below, hookers are usually best advised to incorporate elements of the big-muscle method into their swings if they want to stop their ducks from quacking. Slicers, on the other hand, are usually best advised to incorporate elements of the small-muscle method into their swings if they want to straighten out their banana balls. Your age, flexibility, and body type are also important considerations in deciding which swings you are actually capable of executing.

As in learning how to improve your putting, the first step in learning how to improve your full swing is to evaluate the available options. But to make an objective determination of which swing method and which swing instructor is "perfect" for you and your golfing goals, you need to be equipped with some core knowledge that applies to every type of golf swing and every type of ball flight from hooks to slices.

▶ The Moment of Truth

What is the primary purpose of any golf swing?

Ask just about any great golfer or any great golf instructor, and you'll get essentially the same answer. It all boils down to what happens when the golf club makes impact with the golf ball. That is why impact is often called "the moment of truth." In his book *The Golf Swing Simplified,* British teaching pro John Jacobs, a former Ryder Cup captain who has been dubbed "the father of European golf," puts it this way: "The golf swing has only one purpose: to deliver the head of the club to the ball correctly."

The immortal Bobby Jones voiced an identical opinion in slightly different words. "The only reason we bother with form and the correct swing," he maintained in *Bobby Jones On Golf,* "is to find the best way of consistently bringing about the proper conditions at impact." Jack Nicklaus concurs. "Whatever any golfer does with a golf club should have only one purpose: to produce correct impact of club on ball," he declares in his book *Golf My Way.* "If he can achieve that consistently, the manner in which he does so doesn't really matter at all."

How do you judge the quality of your impact?

Given the speed of virtually every golf swing, "the moment of truth" is invisible to the naked eye and mostly a blur even with the aid of stop-action video cameras. That being the case, you have to evaluate impact by an indirect measure. Even though it's almost impossible to see what happens at the precise instant the club makes contact with the ball, you can clearly see what happens as a result. The result is the flight of the ball. Jacobs speaks for a large

number of top teaching pros when he emphatically asserts, "The flight of the ball ALWAYS tells you EVERYTHING you need to know to become a better player."

While there is an undeniable truth to that assertion, the task of properly analyzing ball flight can often be much trickier and more complicated than it may appear. Two golfers, or even the same golfer, can hit two successive shots that curve to the right, for example, only to discover that what caused the first shot to curve to the right was very different than what caused the second shot to curve to the right. But you can at least start to get a handle on the causes of your own ball flight by considering four of the five main factors. They are: the angle of the clubface, the point of contact, the path of the swing, and the plane of the swing. (We will consider the fifth factor, the speed of the clubhead, in due course.)

1 The angle of the clubface is the direction in which the club is looking at the moment of impact with the ball. Although all angles are a matter of degree, three basic positions can be described in reference to right-handed golfers, as follows: The clubface can be "open," that is, looking to the right of the target line. The clubface can be "closed," that is, looking to the left of the target. Or the clubface can be "square," that is, looking directly down the target line. Although many variables can influence the angle of the clubface at impact, one of the more important is the way you grip the club. In general, a "weak" grip promotes an open clubface, a "strong" grip

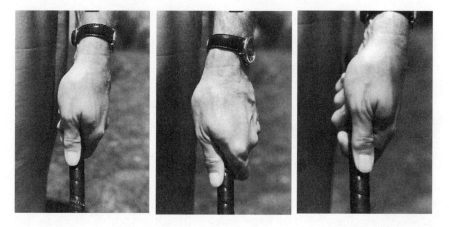

Neutral Grip   *Strong Grip*   *Weak Grip*

promotes a closed clubface, and a "neutral" grip promotes a square clubface.

As Jim McLean often reminds his students, the angle of the clubface is so influential in determining ball flight that it often overrides other factors, including the path of your swing. For example, if you hit a shot from a heavy rough, the grass may twist your clubface into a closed position, causing you to hit a pull hook regardless of whether the path of your swing is outside to inside or inside to outside. McLean calls this phenomenon "clubface override."

2 The point of contact is the position on the clubface at which contact is made with the ball. This is one of the areas where ball flight analysis can get tricky. As in putting, the possibilities include contacting the ball on the center or "sweet spot" of the clubface, contacting the ball on the "heel" of the clubface, and contacting the ball on the "toe" of the clubface. But the results of off-center contacts

made with a driver can be much different and more various than off-center contacts made with a putter.

For example, a ball struck on the toe of a putter is likely to roll to the right, while a ball struck on the toe of a driver is likely to curve to the left. Why? Because the center of gravity on a driver is much farther behind the clubface (and therefore the ball) than the center of gravity on a putter. Similarly, a ball struck on the heel of a putter is likely to roll to the left, while a ball struck on the heel of a driver is likely to curve to the right.

With irons and woods, it is also possible to contact the ball low on the clubface, which may produce a "topped" shot or "thinned" shot on a low trajectory, or to contact the ball high on the clubface, which may produce a "skied" or "pop-up" shot. With irons, there is the further possibility of contacting the ball on the hosel, where the shaft connects with the clubhead, rather than on the clubface; when that occurs, the result is a shank.

3 The path of the swing is the direction along which the club travels en route to the ball relative to the target line. The three main swing path routes are determined by the fact that in golf a player stands to the inside of the ball, facing perpendicular to the target line at address, rather than directly behind the ball, facing down the target line, as in croquet or billiards. The club can travel to the ball on an "inside-to-outside" path relative to the target line. The club can travel on an "outside-to-inside" path relative to the target line. Or the

Square Stance

Closed Stance

Open Stance

club can travel on an "inside-to-square-to-inside" path relative to the target line. Although many variables, including ball position, can influence the path of the swing, one of the more important is your body alignment at address, which can be open, closed, or square to the target line.

4 The plane of the swing is the angle on which the club moves up and down relative to the ball. Most top teaching pros describe the ideal swing plane in reference to the angle formed by the shaft of the club at address, the so-called shaft plane. Ben Hogan visualized a somewhat steeper plane whose angle was formed by a line running up from the ball across the top of his shoulders. Many golfers consciously or unconsciously swing on different planes on their backswings and their downswings. The plane on which the club is actually delivered to the ball is also known as the angle of attack.

Like clubface angles, swing planes are a matter of degree, but generally speaking, you can be in three positions as you deliver the club to the ball on your downswing. You can be "above the plane," which is to say that your angle of attack is steep. You can be "below the plane," which is to say that your angle of attack is shallow. Or you can be "on plane," which is to say that your angle of attack matches the angle of the shaft at address. Apart from any manipulation of the club following your takeaway, some of the more important variables influencing the actual plane of your swing are your posture at address and

the posture or combination of postures you maintain during your backswing and your downswing.

Before leaving the subject of plane, it is important to note that the shaft of a golf club also forms a secondary angle at address, in addition to the shaft plane angle discussed above. This is the forward- or leftward-leaning angle of the shaft created by the design of every club. Of the top-ranked teaching pros, Michael Hebron is particularly keen on emphasizing the significance of the forward-leaning angle. He points out that if the forward-leaning angle is maintained throughout the swing, your hands will be slightly ahead of the ball at impact, thereby allowing you to "compress" the ball effectively. If the forward-leaning angle is converted into a backward-leaning angle by improper manipulation of the club during the swing, your hands will be behind the ball at impact, which means you're likely to hit either the top of the ball or the turf behind the ball.

The Flight of the Ball

The three components of every type of ball flight are direction, distance, and trajectory. As noted above, the trajectory of a shot is directly affected by the point of contact on the clubface—high, low, heel, toe, or center. But trajectory is also affected by the design of your golf clubs. As Alastair Cochran and John Stobbs point out in

their 1968 study *Search for the Perfect Swing,* "In every stroke in golf (apart from some complete mishits and some putts) backspin is applied to the ball." Backspin is created by the club itself, which effectively delivers a glancing blow to the ball as a result of the face being set back according to its respective degree of loft. Backspin is what makes the ball climb into the air until gravity brings it back down.

The curvature of your ball flight is mainly the result of the relative presence or absence of sidespin, which may combine with backspin to tilt or incline the axis on which the ball is spinning. Of the five main factors that affect impact, the angle of your clubface is believed to have the greatest influence on the amount of sidespin applied to the ball, and the direction in which the ball travels. But the path of your swing, the plane of your swing, and the point of contact can also contribute. Assuming that you are not trying to hit the ball backward, your ball flight can take seven basic directional vectors, as illustrated by the chart on page 76.

- ▶ **Straight:** If your clubface is square, your path is inside-to-square-to-inside, and your angle of attack is on plane, your ball will fly straight.

- ▶ **Hook:** If your clubface is closed, your path is inside-to-outside, and your angle of attack is shallow, your ball will curve from right to left.

Seven Basic Types of Ball Flight*

....

STRAIGHT
CLUBFACE: square
PATH: inside-to-square-to-inside
ANGLE OF ATTACK: on plane
BALL FLIGHT: straight toward target

HOOK
CLUBFACE: closed
PATH: inside-to-outside
ANGLE OF ATTACK: shallow
BALL FLIGHT: right to left

SLICE
CLUBFACE: open
PATH: outside-to-inside
ANGLE OF ATTACK: steep
BALL FLIGHT: left to right

PULL
CLUBFACE: square
PATH: outside-to-inside
ANGLE OF ATTACK: steep
BALL FLIGHT: straight left

PUSH
CLUBFACE: square
PATH: inside-to-outside
ANGLE OF ATTACK: shallow
BALL FLIGHT: straight right

PULL HOOK
CLUBFACE: closed
PATH: outside-to-inside
ANGLE OF ATTACK: steep
BALL FLIGHT: starts left, curves left

PUSH SLICE
CLUBFACE: open
PATH: inside-to-outside
ANGLE OF ATTACK: shallow
BALL FLIGHT: starts right, curves right

* Adapted from John Jacobs, *The Golf Swing Simplified* (Buford Books, 1993),
and *Teaching the Game of Golf* (PGA of America, 1998).

▶ **Slice:** If your clubface is open, your path is outside-to-inside, and your angle of attack is steep, your ball will curve from left to right.

▶ **Pull:** If your clubface is square, your path is outside-to-inside, and your angle of attack is steep, your ball will fly straight left.

▶ **Pull hook:** If your clubface is closed, your path is outside-to-inside, and your angle of attack is steep, your ball will start left and curve farther left.

▶ **Push:** If your clubface is square, your path is inside-to-outside, and your angle of attack is shallow, your ball will fly straight right.

▶ **Push slice:** If your clubface is open, with the path and angle of attack of a push, your ball will start right and curve farther right.

The speed of the clubhead, the fifth factor affecting quality of impact, influences the distance your ball travels. As most top teaching pros would hasten to remind, the angle of your clubface, the point of contact, the path of your swing, and your angle of attack can also affect distance and/or clubhead speed in myriad ways. A low running hook created by a closed clubface, for example, will generally travel a longer distance than a ballooning slice created by an open clubface. Swinging the club on plane and on an inside-to-square-to-

*"The Moment of Truth"—All swing methods
aim to create ideal conditions at impact.*

inside path will typically allow you to swing more freely and to create
more clubhead speed than other plane and path combinations.

That said, the speed of your clubhead at impact is a result of
the way your swing utilizes and coordinates the two halves of your
physique—your upper body and your lower body. For our purposes,

your upper body can be defined as everything above your waist, including your shoulders, arms, wrists, hands, and the upper portion of your torso. Your lower body can be defined as everything below the waist, including your lower torso, hips, legs, knees, and feet. If your clubface angle, path, and plane are predetermined mainly by elements of your setup such as grip, alignment, and posture, your clubhead speed is determined by the ways your upper body and lower body actually move during your swing.

The debate over the proper roles of the upper body and the lower body in swinging a golf club is as old as the game of golf, and it strikes at the heart of the features that distinguish one swing method from another. In recent years, the debate has kept pace with the evolution of swing methods. Most teaching pros now recast it in terms of the body versus the hands and arms, or in terms of big muscles versus small muscles.

Small-Muscle, Big-Muscle, and Mixed-Muscle Swings

Just as every golf swing must somehow involve both your upper body and your lower body, every golf swing must somehow involve both your small-muscles and your big muscles. The difference between the leading swing methods currently in use on the professional tours is a matter of emphasis and orientation. Which set of muscles actively starts and controls the backswing, and which set

remains relatively passive? Which set of muscles actively starts and controls the downswing, and which set remains relatively passive? Which set of muscles is in the driver's seat at impact?

1 The small-muscle swing is the oldest method on the evolutionary chain, and still the method most widely recommended for today's recreational golfers. The small-muscle method traces back to the late nineteenth and early twentieth centuries, the era of players like "Old Tom" Morris, who pioneered the long, flat, body-swaying "St. Andrews swing," and Harry Vardon, who pioneered the somewhat more upright, more compact, and more spine-centered "English method." Because golf clubs were made with extremely whippy hickory shafts, golfers had to manipulate the small muscles of their forearms, wrists, and hands to generate power and square the club-face through impact.

The advent of stiffer metal shafts in the 1930s prompted the likes of Byron Nelson to develop a new form of small-muscle swing. Unlike the St. Andrews swing and the English method, which featured early wrist-cocking on the backswing, Nelson's swing featured a "one-piece" takeaway in which the shoulders, arms, and hands moved back together as a unit. But the new, easier-to-control steel shafts allowed Nelson to make greater use of his knees and legs to generate power and square the clubface. He maintained a noticeable flex in his left knee both on his backswing and through impact. As

the writer Dick Aultman observes in *The Methods of Golf's Masters,* "Instead of hitting 'against' his left side, Nelson hit *with* his left side."

With the notable exceptions of Hogan and Snead, whose motions contained elements of the big-muscle swing, the majority of top touring pros used a fairly pure version of the small-muscle swing right through the late 1970s. Among the leading exemplars of the small-muscle method were the young Jack Nicklaus and Johnny Miller. Their swings featured Nelson's flexed left knee and leg drive through impact accompanied by a rolling of the forearms, hands, and wrists.

The contemporary version of the small-muscle swing method still emphasizes the role of the hands and arms as sources of feel, and as the controlling forces in governing clubface angle, path, plane, and clubhead speed, with the body merely reacting to the initiating movements of the hands and arms throughout the backswing and downswing. In contrast to earlier versions, however, the legs remain relatively passive, providing a firm base for the torso and upper body without driving through impact in the flexed-knee style of Nelson. The leading advocates of the small-muscle method among the top ten teaching pros are Jim Flick, coproprietor of the Nicklaus/Flick golf schools, and Bob Toski.

While the small-muscle method is sometimes disdained as old-fashioned, it continues to weather the test of time. That is because it was developed and refined primarily in golf schools

geared to average golfers. The vast majority of average golfers are slicers. Most instructors who teach average golfers report that students who slice the ball appear to improve faster and more easily by emulating small-muscle rather than big-muscle swing techniques.

Why does the small-muscle method seem to be so effective in curing a slice? The answer can be found in a slicer's ball flight, which typically results from an open clubface combined with an outside-to-inside path and a steep angle of attack. Oftentimes the root cause of these clubface, path, and plane errors is a slicer's tendency to overuse or improperly use his body, and underuse or improperly use his hands and arms. Among the more common mistakes are the "sway," in which the slicer's weight slides outside his right leg on the backswing, and the "reverse pivot," in which the slicer's weight revolves around his left leg on the backswing. The downswing typically consists of either a body slide back to the ball or a body lunge that flings the club around and "over the top."

Flick and other pros who advocate the small-muscle method claim that encouraging their students to focus on more active use of their hands and arms during their swings has two beneficial effects. First, it helps "quiet" their body motion and center their swings around the axis of their spines, thereby reducing sways and reverse pivots that lead to outside-to-inside swing paths and swing planes that are too steep. Secondly, it provides a direct means to square and release the clubhead through impact, thereby reducing open clubface errors.

Critics of the small-muscle swing claim that it is a high-maintenance method that is low on power and consistency. By using the hands, wrists, and arms to control the swing, they contend, a golfer introduces too many actively moving parts to what should be a relatively simple motion. Likewise, releasing the club through impact demands precise timing that can be achieved only through hours of practice. And by definition, the small-muscle method allegedly fails to fully utilize the larger muscles of the body, which are stronger and purportedly more reliable under pressure.

2 The big-muscle swing, also known as the modern swing, developed partly as a response to the perceived inadequacies of the small-muscle swing. It began to gain increasing acceptance with the introduction of stiffer steel and graphite shafts in the early and middle 1980s. Where the traditions of the small-muscle method were carried on by golf instructors who taught mostly recreational players, the big-muscle method was developed and refined by golf instructors who worked mostly with tour players.

One of the recognized pioneers of the big-muscle method is top-ten teaching pro Jimmy Ballard, who has tutored the likes of Jim Colbert, Hal Sutton, and Jesper Parnevik. Ballard has been teaching big-muscle methods since the early 1970s. He set forth the basic concept of maintaining a "connection" between the body and the

hands and arms in his 1981 manual *How to Perfect Your Golf Swing*, the basis of which he admittedly derived from his own mentor Sam Byrd, a former major-league baseball player turned professional golfer. But it was David Leadbetter and his protégé Nick Faldo, winner of three Masters and three British Opens, who subsequently popularized the big-muscle method in the media and among the golfing masses.

In contrast to the small-muscle method, the big-muscle method assigns a relatively passive role to the hands, wrists, and arms. Instead, it relies on the rotation of the larger muscles of the torso to generate power and to square the clubface. Ballard summarizes the differences between the big-muscle method's reliance on the body as opposed to the small-muscle method's reliance on the hands and arms with one of his patented homespun metaphors: "We believe that the dog wags the tail—the tail doesn't wag the dog."

Of course, not all big-muscle methods are identical in every respect. As far as the backswing is concerned, Ballard and Leadbetter agree that the role of the lower body is mainly to provide a solid base, with the hips resisting turn to create coil as you load your weight onto your right side with a lateral movement of your upper torso. But they part company in their prescriptions for the downswing. Ballard maintains that the downswing should be initiated by the right leg, and that you should "fire" your entire right side through impact. In his book *The Golf Swing*, Leadbetter maintains that the downswing

should be triggered by a diagonal movement of your left knee, and that you should "focus on keeping your right heel on the ground until it is pulled off by the unwinding of your torso."

Many top teaching pros who personally favor the big-muscle method are quick to warn their students that it is, as its developmental history suggests, more suited to tour pros and other highly skilled players than to average golfers. That is because most highly skilled players are hookers rather than slicers. They tend to overuse or improperly use their hands and arms, and underuse or improperly use their bodies. In emphasizing the role of the body, the big-muscle method often provides the needed counterbalance. As Hank Haney puts it in *The Only Golf Lesson You'll Ever Need*, "Great players fight a hook because they have fast hands. . . . So they focus on the body. They feel like they need to get the body to go along with the hands and arms to (a) get their timing right and (b) get the feeling of taking their hands 'out' of the swing."

Critics of the big-muscle swing focus on many of the same points that advocates cite as advantages, namely, that it is a method not easily mastered by average golfers, and that it assumes you already have sufficiently—or more than sufficiently—active hands. Jim Flick summed up the critique during a debate with Jimmy Ballard at the 1998 PGA Teaching and Coaching Summit: "I want a swing that's compatible with the full swing and the short game, which is teaching the hands and arms to feel and sense the path the club is taking, the

angle of approach, [and] the speed [of] the club. . . . If you get away from that by being overly concerned with what your body is doing, you're interfering with your chance of building feel for the golf club."

3 The mixed-muscle swing method is a kind of postmodern hybrid of the small-muscle and big-muscle methods. Advocates generally fall into two camps. One camp consists of teaching pros like Rick Smith, who takes an admittedly eclectic approach to golf instruction. When asked whether small muscles or big muscles should be dominant, Smith quickly replies, "Both." His reasoning is based on the incontrovertible fact that both sets of muscles must participate in some fashion in every golf swing. Depending on the student, Smith adjusts his emphasis to achieve what he describes as a "matching" or coordination of small-muscle and big-muscle action.

The other mixed-muscle camp consists of teaching pros like Butch Harmon and his star pupil, Tiger Woods. Like Smith, Harmon believes that every golf swing should incorporate both big muscles and small muscles. But when Woods asked for help in gaining more consistency and distance control following his victory in the 1997 Masters, Harmon added some new twists on traditional techniques that required Woods to embark on his now-famous conditioning regimen.

Among the changes Woods made under Harmon's tutelage were restricting his hip turn and slightly reducing the length of his arm swing on the way back. He also worked on slowing the speed of

his torso rotation, and keeping his left wrist bowed through impact. These crucial refinements allow Woods to hold the clubface square to the target line a split second longer than before, resulting in a powerful but tightly controlled ball flight that might best be described as a relatively low trajectory punch shot that stops on the green like a high-lofted spin shot.

The variations on the postmodern mixed-muscle swing developed by Harmon and Woods should probably come with a warning label: "Don't Try This at Home." Although it's certainly possible for an average golfer to master the rudiments of the Woods punch, only a player who possesses his athleticism and the powerful forearms he has developed in his conditioning regimen can even hope to hit 280-yard stingers with a two iron. Then again, it may be worth giving the mixed-muscle method a try if you've set your sights on duplicating or surpassing Woods's feat of winning four major championships in a row.

Biomechanical Methods

With advances in computer technology and kinetic research, several biomechanical approaches to golf instruction have gained popularity over the past decade. Biomechanics is a fancy term for the study of human movement. The potential range of movement obviously varies from individual to individual according to factors such as age,

strength, flexibility, and type of physique. But one of the basic premises of biomechanics is that the ways we actually can and do move are governed by the ways our joints and spine are intended to work. In most biomechanical models of golf instruction, the human body is seen as a machine whose ability to swing a golf club in the most efficient manner is dictated by certain inherent design capabilities and limitations.

One biomechanical approach is represented by the computerized graphic of the so-called **ModelPro swing** that some television broadcasters have recently used as a standard against which to compare the swings of PGA Tour players. The ModelPro was developed by Dr. Ralph Mann, a former Olympic hurdler with a Ph.D. in biomechanics, and Fred Griffin, one of *Golf Magazine*'s top one hundred teaching pros. It is based on films of more than one hundred top tour pros, including Jack Nicklaus, Jesper Parnevik, Davis Love III, and Mark O'Meara.

Mann and Griffin state on their Web site that "the ModelPro is much more than a simple average of these elite golfers. Rather, we have used statistics to isolate the best of their common characteristics while rejecting their individual weaknesses." As a result, they claim that their model "not only has a biomechanically perfect game but also the perfect balance of strength, flexibility, and coordination."

The advantage of ModelPro is that it provides an ideal swing to which golfers can compare their own swings. Advocates on the pro

tours report that such comparisons help them isolate and focus on their own individual strengths and weaknesses. The disadvantage of the ModelPro is that it is an ideal based on a computer-generated composite that few if any human beings can hope to match on a one-for-one basis. Mann and Griffin report that the human being whose swing comes closest to the ModelPro swing is, not surprisingly, Tiger Woods.

Another leading proponent of biomechanical methods is Rick Martino, director of instruction for the PGA of America, who ranks nineteenth in the *Golf Digest* poll of top teaching pros. According to Martino, our ankles, knees, elbows, and wrists are designed to operate as vertical hinges that move up and down, while our shoulders and hips are designed to operate as rotary joints that turn. The role of the spine, which Martino refers to as a "stack joint," is to provide forward bending and side tilt to the left and right. He warns that golfers get into trouble when they attempt to use their joints contrary to design, which includes such common errors as breaking the ideal backswing plane by rotating wrists and elbows rather than remaining on plane by allowing them to hinge up and down.

Martino believes that the most efficient golf swing is one that creates power through the coiling of the body in conjunction with biomechanically "correct" movements of the wrists, arms, and shoulders. He says that the takeaway should be initiated by a diagonal move from the center of your torso that makes your right hip socket "sit" over your right heel. Once you have rotated your shoul-

ders 90 degrees on your backswing, you should start the change of direction by moving your left hip socket over your left heel. That, in turn, should set off a chain reaction in which your arms come straight down and your spine angle changes from a slight left tilt to a right tilt that brings the club toward the ball on an inside path. You now rotate your body through impact while simultaneously extending your right arm in a downward, outward, and forward motion.

Among the advantages of Martino's biomechanical approach are the clarity and precision with which the movements in a golf swing are assigned to various body parts. Likewise, it incorporates both big muscles and small muscles in well-defined roles. Critics say the disadvantage is that this basic prescription, though open to personalized modifications, may be too mechanical and standardized. Our joints may operate as hinges, but we are also living organisms with an infinite variety of body styles, not uniformly designed machines.

The LAWs of Golf system is a third biomechanical approach to golf instruction that departs significantly from those of Martino, Mann, and Griffin. The acronym LAW stands for the system's three basic swing paradigms: leverage, arc, and width. The paradigms were developed by two top-twenty teaching pros, Mike Adams and Dr. Jim Suttie, and their associate, T. J. Tomasi, as an antidote to conventional one-swing-fits-all approaches. The basic thesis of the LAWs of Golf is that, given that every golfer is different in body type and physique, every golfer should have his own swing, appropriate to his body type and physique (see chart on page 91).

Testing the LAWs of Golf

How to Match Your Swing Type to Your Body Type

• • • • • • • • • • • • • • • •

Mike Adams, T. J. Tomasi, and Jim Suttie have devised the LAWs Identification Tests to help their students match their swing types to their body types. Here are three of those tests that you can do at home to find out if you're a Leverage, Arc, or Width player.

1   ARM ELEVATION TEST: Stand against a wall with both shoulder blades touching the wall and your arms hanging by your sides. Make a pistol with your right hand and raise your right arm toward your right shoulder, keeping it snug against your rib cage.

Leverage: Your thumb is about even with the top of your shoulder.

Arc: Your thumb is above the top of your shoulder.

Width: Your thumb is below the top of your shoulder.

L.A.W.s of Golf:
Arm Elevation Test

2   ARM SWING TEST: Stand against a wall with both shoulder blades touching the wall, and extend both arms straight out in front of you so they are parallel to the floor. Now swing your left arm to the right and stop as soon as the upper portion of your bicep rubs against your chest.

L.A.W.s of Golf:
Arm Swing Test

(continued)

Leverage: Your hands meet as your left arm stops against your chest.

Arc: Your hands cross before your left arm meets your chest.

Width: Your left arm stops against your chest before your hands meet.

3   **Shoulder Flexibility Test: Stand with your right shoulder against the inside of a doorjamb, and raise your right hand so that your elbow and shoulder are level as if you are taking an oath. Now rotate your right forearm back as far as you can without hurting yourself.**

Leverage: Your forearm rotates to or just past vertical.

L.A.W.s of Golf: Shoulder Flexibility Test

Arc: Your forearm rotates well past vertical.

Width: Your forearm is unable to rotate to vertical.

• •

Greg Norman, Davis Love III, and Craig Stadler are near-perfect illustrations of what the LAWs of Golf system is all about. Norman has a "leverage" swing that relies on the creation of depth, angles, and leverage. Like his evenly proportioned mesomorphic physique, it is a paragon of balance with an even tempo. Love has an "arc" swing that relies on the long arms of his thin-chested ectomorphic physique to create height on his backswing. He has a slow tempo that enables him to utilize his enormous wingspan. Stadler has a "width" swing that relies on the muscular power of his thick-chested endomorphic physique. He hits at the ball with a short, quick tempo.

The implications of the LAWs of Golf for what Adams, Suttie, and Tomasi believe to be biomechanically suitable swing instruction are profound. They are also somewhat unconventional. They apply many of the familiar dictums common to traditional golf teaching programs, but the difference is that they don't apply all of them to all comers. And they often recommend changes in grip, posture, stance, backswing, and downswing that are marked departures from "standard" advice.

The leverage swing closely resembles the modern big-muscle swing advocated by the likes of David Leadbetter. Here the dominant power source is mechanical advantage provided by leverage and the creation of angles between the shaft and the hands and arms, and the overall look of the swing motion is whirling and rotational. But what is magic for arc or width players can be tragic for leverage players. Leverage players, for example, are advised to forget about attempting a classic "one-piece" takeaway, in which the club starts back with the simultaneous movement of shoulders, arms, hands, and hips, and the wrist cock is deliberately delayed. Instead, leverage players are encouraged to start the club back with their arms close to their chests and to cock their wrist quickly to create angles.

The dominant power source for arc players is positional advantage created by the circumference and height of the swing arc, and the overall look of the swing resembles a slinging motion. In contrast to leverage players, arc players are advised to make a one-piece

takeaway and to delay their wrist cock to gain height on the back-swing. But arc players are also encouraged to employ plenty of lateral leg action to prevent the club from getting trapped behind them on the downswing, and to finish with their hands high and their backs in the old-fashioned reverse-C posture now disparaged by most other teaching pros.

Width players must rely on the muscular advantage provided by their physical strength. Rather than emulating the classic features of a leverage swing, they are encouraged to get the most out of their nonclassic "punchy"-looking motions by maximizing the width of their backswings. Where classic form calls for a square stance and a still head, they are directed to drop their right foot back in a "closed" stance, and to let their head "float" toward their right knee. They are also taught to set the club on a more upright plane, with a wrist-cocking action that resembles a "stiff-arm" in football.

The advantage of the LAWs of Golf system is that it provides an alternative to instructional approaches that encourage every player to swing with one particular method, regardless of his physical characteristics. Although many other golf instructors have consciously or unconsciously adapted their teaching to the individual body types of their students, Adams, Suttie, and Tomasi are the first to formalize the matching of body types and swing types into a coherent system. The disadvantage of the LAWs system lies in the difficulty of actually pinpointing which of the three swings or com-

binations thereof is right for you, especially if you have a hybrid physique that is suited to a hybrid swing style.

Golf Swings of the Future

Armchair historians of golf are fond of pointing out that for all the advances in equipment and technology, the elements of a sound swing have changed relatively little over the past century. That is true, depending on how you define the elements of a sound swing. Harry Vardon certainly tried to achieve the same basic conditions at impact that Tiger Woods does today, namely, an angle of attack that is on plane, a square clubface, and contact with the ball on the sweet spot.

David Lee believes the golf swings of the future will differ from those of the past in at least one crucial respect—the absence of a conventional backswing. Lee, who has long been ranked on *Golf Magazine's* list of America's top one hundred teaching pros, is the father of the so-called **Gravity Golf system.** As his teaching philosophy and swing method would suggest, Lee is a proudly unorthodox man who occupies the experimental fringes of contemporary golf instruction. But he is quick to point out that no less a traditionalist than Johnny Miller has also predicted that the golf swing of the future will have no backswing, as we now know it. Likewise, mainstream big-muscle advocate David Leadbetter recently debuted a "golf swing of the future," which eliminates a conventional take-

Gravity Golf Swing: Takeaway

away move in favor of pre-setting the club at a waist-high position and starting the backswing from there.

The Gravity Golf system developed by Lee actually features two swings, a for-now version and a futuristic version. He claims that the for-now version is derived in part from the swings of Fred Couples and the young Jack Nicklaus. It starts from a conventional address position, with the clubhead placed behind the ball. You initiate your swing by firming your arms and then "heaving" the club back with a one-piece motion of your back and shoulders. At approximately eighteen inches into the backswing, you hit what Lee calls "the first release," where you release all tension in your hands and arms, allowing the club to travel to the top of the backswing on momentum alone. But instead of keeping your right elbow pointed down at the ground, you allow it to point behind you or "fly," as Nicklaus and Couples do.

In the for-now version of the Gravity Golf swing, your downswing is initiated primarily by the forces of gravity. As the club head reaches the top of its backswing arc, your body "falls" to the left, or parallel to the target line, thanks in part to the leveraged resistance of your right leg and your "flying" right elbow, which folds downward. The next key move is what Lee calls the "counter fall," which is similar to a tennis player leaning backward in a serving motion or a water-skier leaning backward from the tow rope. In the counter fall, your weight moves toward your left heel at an

angle 70 degrees left of the target line to offset the rightward or outward-traveling weight of the club and your arms moving toward the ball. As you complete the counter fall, you simply rotate your left hip through impact.

The futuristic version of the Gravity Golf swing is intended to eliminate the timing required by conventional backswings by eliminating the backswing itself. You start with the club positioned behind the ball at address, but rather than swinging it backward, you lift it straight up in what Lee calls a "referenced up route" so that the shaft is perpendicular to the ground, and the butt end of the grip is even with the top of your forehead. Both arms remain slightly flexed, so your right elbow will be able to "fly." Then you simply turn your shoulders to the right to move the club to the top of the backswing. From there, the resistance of your angled right leg launches you into the sequence of fall, counter fall, and left hip rotation.

Critics of the Gravity Golf system point out that none of the leading tour pros has ever used Lee's golf swing of the future in competition. But for all their unorthodox features, both the futuristic and for-now versions of the Gravity Golf swing contain elements that many other top-ranked teaching pros endorse. They include the one-piece takeaway recommended for arc players in the LAWs system, the "first release" of tension recommended in some form or fashion by most golf instructors and dramatized in Nicklaus's backswing, and the fall and counter fall evident in Couples's seemingly effortless downswing.

Natural Golf is another nonconventional method that has recently gained public interest, thanks in part to a national advertising campaign and endorsements from former PGA-champion-turned-television-commentator Bob Rosburg and European touring pro Sandy Lyle. Natural Golf schools are under the direction of Ed Woronicz, a veteran PGA of America member, but the method is based on the swing of Murray "Moe" Norman, a highly eccentric former Canadian Amateur champion known for his remarkable ball-striking prowess. In addition to a string of non–PGA Tour victories, Norman's accomplishments include shooting an eighteen hole score of 59 three times in competitions.

In contrast to conventional approaches, the Natural Golf system calls for gripping the club in the palm, as opposed to the fingers of your right hand, with your right forearm aligned behind the shaft. The setup position features a wider-than-standard stance and a high hand position, which combine to create an almost stiff-armed, reaching look at address. The prescribed backswing bears some similarly to the width swing in the LAWs of Golf system in that it is deliberately short, with the hands never moving above shoulder height and the shaft of the club never becoming parallel to the ground. The prescribed forward swing calls for keeping both feet on the ground and your body facing the ball through the impact zone, with as little hip rotation as possible.

Proponents of the Natural Golf system claim it offers both greater accuracy and more power than conventional approaches because its

"Square Tracking" action promotes more solid contact with the ball by eliminating the need to rotate forearms and hips away from the target line during the backswing and then back onto the target line during the forward swing. Critics of Natural Golf note that no top-ranked pros or amateurs save Norman and Lyle use such a method. They also contend that it sacrifices distance for the sake of accuracy by limiting the input of major power sources such as forearm rotation, hip rotation, and backswing length, though some concede it may be suitable for golfers like Norman who have short-armed, barrel-chested physiques and rely on muscular power to generate clubhead speed.

Finding Your "Perfect" Swing

The ill-fated experiences of many great players confirm that the search for "the perfect golf swing" typically leads to frustration and disappointment. The fact is, however, that you can still find a golf swing that is perfect for you and your own golfing goals. The swing methods currently used by PGA Tour and top-ranked amateur players have evolved along with advances in equipment and with the help of video technology used in instruction. Average golfers can make major strides toward improving their games and lowering their handicaps by judiciously weighing and selecting among the available options, and by playing with clubs that fit them (see appendix D).

The three leading swing methods, viewed from an historical perspective, differ primarily in their respective emphasis on the role of the body versus the hands and arms. The small-muscle method, which emphasizes the role of the hands and arms, may be best suited to average golfers who slice the ball. The big-muscle method, which emphasizes the role of the body, may be best suited for advanced players who hook the ball. The postmodern mixed-muscle method, which emphasizes the coordination of small-muscle and big-muscle action, can be suitable for a wide variety of golfers, though the variations developed for Tiger Woods are probably best reserved for a rare gifted few.

The leading swing methods, viewed from the biomechanical perspective, differ according to their emphasis on ideal paradigms and/or a golfer's body type. The basic biomechanical methods advocated by the likes of ModelPro computer graphic simulation developers Ralph Mann and Fred Griffin and PGA of America director of instruction Rick Martino maintain that the human body functions much like a machine, with inherent design capabilities and limitations that dictate the most efficient way to swing a golf club. In the LAWs of Golf system, the shape of your physique is far more important than the shape of your ball flight. Both hookers and slicers need to be concerned primarily with whether they are leverage players with average physiques, arc players with long-limbed physiques, or width players with thick-chested physiques.

The Gravity Golf system offers two swings, a for-now version and a futuristic version, which emphasize the release of muscular tension in the takeaway and the use of gravity in delivering the club-head to the ball. Both despite and because of their unorthodox features, the Gravity Golf swings may appeal to hookers and slicers who are dissatisfied with conventional swing methods. The same may be said of the Natural Golf system based on the Moe Norman swing, which deliberately limits backswing length, forearm rotation, and hip rotation.

Just as putting is subject to wide individual variations, every player's golf swing will ultimately turn out to be as unique as his fingerprints, no matter what method he chooses to emulate. The differences between small-, big-, and mixed-muscle swings, conventional techniques and unorthodox techniques, can be both subtle and significant. But the ultimate aim of all of them is the same. "The goal with everybody's swing, regardless of ability," David Leadbetter noted in a recent *Golf Digest* article analyzing Tiger Woods's swing, "is to get the right blend of arm swing and body motion, so that through impact these two components match up."

The swing method that is perfect for you and your golfing goals is the one that best enables you to consistently produce the correct impact of club on ball. It does not matter how it looks or who else uses that method. All that matters is that it works. As we will discuss in chapter 6, the best way to go about finding your swing is

with the help of a competent and trusted instructor, but the choice is ultimately up to you. The important thing is to make a choice and stick with it. Otherwise, you're likely to drive yourself nuts before you figure out how to drive a ball in the fairway.

SUMMARY: *Top Teaching Pros and Their Full-Swing Methods*

▶ SMALL-MUSCLE METHOD

The traditional small-muscle method emphasizes the role of the hands and arms (as opposed to the body) in controlling the swing. Advocates claim it is the most effective method for curing a slice because slicers overuse body action and underuse hands and arms. Recommend for beginners and average golfers, most of whom slice the ball.

Jim Flick, Bob Toski

▶ BIG-MUSCLE METHOD

The modern big-muscle method emphasizes the role of the body (as opposed to hands and arms) in controlling the swing. Advocates claim it is the most effective method for curing a hook because hookers overuse hands and arms and underuse body action. Recommended for advanced players.

Jimmy Ballard, Michael Hebron, David Leadbetter, Jim McLean

▶Mixed-Muscle Method

The postmodern mixed-muscle method emphasis coordination of body action and hand and arm action so they "match"; recommended for all ability levels. Postmodern variations developed for Tiger Woods require exceptional coordination and strength; recommended for a gifted few.

Chuck Cook, Hank Haney, Butch Harmon, Rick Smith

▶Biomechanical Methods

Biomechanical methods aim to prescribe the most efficient golf swing based on correct movements of the joints and spine. The ModelPro swing uses film and statistics to offer a computer-generated graphic ideal swing. The LAWs of Golf system, derived from biomechanical studies, matches swing methods to individual body types—leverage swing prescribed for average physiques; arc swing prescribed for long-armed, flexible physiques; width swing prescribed for short-armed, muscular physiques.

Mike Adams, Dr. Jim Suttie, T. J. Tomasi (LAWs of Golf),

Dr. Ralph Mann, Fred Griffin (ModelPro), Rick Martino

The Gravity Golf system features two swings based on gravity, momentum, and rotation. The for-now version, patterned after the swings of Fred Couples and Jack Nicklaus, emphasizes release of tension, fall, and "counter fall." The futuristic version features a "referenced up route" takeaway that eliminates a conventional backswing. The Natural Golf system, based on the swing of Canadian legend Moe Norman, deliberately limits forearm rotation, hip rotation, and backswing length to promote a "Square Tracking" action. Recommended for golfers dissatisfied with traditional methods.

David Lee (Gravity Golf), Ed Woronicz (Natural Golf)

4 FORMULATE A FEEL:
Picking Your Approach to the Short Game

"Drive for show, putt for dough" is one of the oldest clichés in golf, but it omits any reference to what many pros regard as the real magic stick. Although Ben Hogan and Harvey Penick disagreed about whether the putter was more important than the driver, they both counted the wedge as one of the three indispensable clubs in the bag. The wedge is the primary tool of the short game. And the short game, which can be defined as any and all shots within 100 yards of the green, is often what enables you to convert the drive you hit for show into a putt you can make for dough—which in my case, and probably in yours, means the shorter the putt, the better.

"In golf, how you play inside of 100 yards is the prime determinant of how you score," declares short-game guru Dave Pelz.

"We all spend time pounding range balls and trying to find the perfect groove so we can hit pure shots," two-time U.S. Open champion Lee Janzen notes in his foreword to Pelz's *Short Game Bible,*

"but our most valuable time is spent working on shots from 100 yards into the greens."

Why do top players and top teaching pros say the short game is so crucial to scoring? Just look at the PGA Tour statistics for greens in regulation. The ten leaders in that category hit 70 to 75 percent of greens in regulation, or roughly 12 to 13 greens per round. The rest of the top 125 players on the tour hit about 65 percent of greens in regulation, or between 11 and 12 greens per round. In other words, even the best players in the world will have to get up and down to save par on at least 5 and as many as 7 holes per round. And that's on an average day. Under adverse playing conditions, the number of par-saving situations is often much, much higher.

"I won the [1986 U.S.] Open with my short game, on one day, in fact," Raymond Floyd reports in his instructional manual *From 60 Yards In: How to Master Golf's Short Game.* "In the opening round on Thursday, we played in what may have been the worst weather I've ever encountered—cold, rainy, and the wind howling. . . . I had no feel whatsoever for the full shots and hit them terribly. . . . [But] I shot 75, and . . . finished only five shots behind the leader on a day when the average score was 78.1. And mine could have been an 85. I took only 25 putts. My pitching, chipping, and putting saved me."

If the short game is of prime importance to the pros, it is, as Floyd observes, "doubly important to the amateurs." Why? Because amateurs, especially high and middle handicappers, hit fewer

greens in regulation than the pros. As a result, they face more short-game shots per round. Pelz reports that his proprietary studies show that 60 to 65 percent of all shots are played from inside 100 yards. That includes approach shots to short par fours and par fives not reached in two shots, as well as putts.

While Pelz's critics may challenge the accuracy of his statistics, he and his fellow top-ten teaching pros unanimously agree that the majority of their students woefully neglect their short games. Most amateurs spend about 90 percent of their practice time working on their full swings, and only about 10 percent of their practice time, if that, working on their short games. Among PGA Tour pros, especially the leading money winners, those percentages are often reversed. As Tiger Woods's coach, Butch Harmon, observes, for the pros, "practicing the short game is almost a religion."

The three main components of the short game are pitch shots, chip shots, and bunker shots. Generally speaking, a pitch is a high-lofted shot in which the ball spends more time in the air than on the ground. A chip is a low-running shot in which the ball spends more time on the ground than in the air. And a bunker shot is any of several types of shots needed to extricate the ball from lies in sand.

Perhaps not surprisingly, the differences between the leading short-game methods are often mirror images of the differences between the leading putting methods and the leading full-swing methods. That's because short-game shots typically incorporate or

combine certain elements of putting techniques and certain elements of full-swing techniques.

But what fundamentally distinguishes one approach to the short game from another is whether the instructor advocates a **unified-swing theory** or a **multiple-swing theory.**" Advocates of the unified-swing theory maintain that short-game shots are basically miniature versions of a full swing and/or a putting stroke. Advocates of the multiple-swing theory insist that the short game demands a completely different set of motions than those used on full shots and putts.

So how do you go about choosing the short-game method that is "perfect" for you?

The process is basically the same as choosing between putting methods and full-swing methods, with an added allowance for individual capabilities. For once, both hookers and slicers are pretty much in the same boat. You can learn the same short-game methods and techniques regardless of whether your full shots tend to curve to the left or to the right. But if ball flight is not one of the primary determining factors, your age, flexibility, strength, experience, and overall playing ability often are. A shot that one golfer can execute with a half swing of a sand wedge, for example, may be a full-pitching wedge shot for another golfer.

The first step in learning how to improve your short game is to evaluate the available short-game options as objectively as possible.

The next steps are to pick the method best suited to you and your golfing goals, to pick an instructor who can teach that method effectively, and then to stick with your chosen method and instructor.

It is vitally important to remember that in the short game, as in putting, accuracy is paramount. The amount of power you can muster for a short-game shot is, with rare exceptions, of little or no consequence. What matters is your touch, which is really just another word for accuracy in distance and direction. Many of the leading short-game methods, be they unified-swing or multiple-swing approaches, offer formulas for calibrating the distance of short-game shots. Others emphasize feel over formulas. But all of the leading short-game methods rely on the same primary tool—the magic stick called the wedge—about which you need to have some basic core knowledge.

A Few Words About Wedges

Once upon a time, there was no such thing as a wedge. The old-fashioned sets of golf clubs used by the likes of Old Tom Morris and Harry Vardon in centuries gone by included a "lofting iron," which was the rough equivalent of the modern-day eight iron, and a "niblick," which was the equivalent of the modern-day nine iron. These clubs had lofts that ranged from about 49 degrees to about 44 degrees, and they were the principal tools golfers used to play shots from within 100 yards of the green.

One of the first sand wedges was used by the American pro Horton Smith in the 1920s. Designed by E. M. MacClain of Houston, Texas, the revolutionary club had a concave face that made it ideal for scooping balls out of bunkers, but it was banned by the United States Golf Association in 1931. Gene Sarazen, the shoemaker's son known as "the Squire," is credited with inventing the forerunner of the modern sand wedge. It had a heavy blade with a straight face that conformed with USGA regulations. After Sarazen won both the British Open and the U.S. Open in 1932, the Squire's sand wedge became a staple in the bags of his golfing rivals.

Most contemporary tour pros and top amateurs now carry at least three wedges in their bags. The typical club set includes a pitching wedge, with lofts ranging from 47 degrees to 49 degrees; a sand wedge, with lofts ranging from 54 degrees to 56 degrees; and a lob wedge, with a loft of 59 degrees or more. In recent years, a number of players have added a fourth wedge. Some carry "gap" wedges with lofts ranging from 51 degrees to 53 degrees. A few carry extra lofted wedges with lofts as high as 64 or 65 degrees (see illustration on page 114).

The main purposes of these three- and four-wedge configurations are to enhance distance control and trajectory control so as to enable the player to have a variety of shot-making options. As noted in chapter 3, virtually every stroke played in golf applies backspin to the ball. Backspin makes a ball carry through the air and helps a ball

stop on the green. Although there are various techniques for increasing backspin on wedge shots, the wedge itself will do the majority of the work for you thanks to its design. Remember, backspin is created because the club delivers a glancing blow to the ball, and this is because the face is set back according to its respective degree of loft. The higher the degree of loft, the greater amount of backspin imparted to the ball.

The range of lofts in the wedges the pros carry are not random. In most cases, they select a set of wedges that have evenly spaced differences in lofts—for example, a 48-degree pitching wedge, a 52-degree gap wedge, and a 56-degree sand wedge. Through experimentation on the practice tee and on the golf course, they know exactly how far (distance) and how high or low (trajectory) they can hit each wedge with a full swing, a three-quarter swing, or a half swing. If there is some overlap between the distances achieved using a full swing with a high-lofted wedge and a half swing with a lower-lofted wedge, that is all the better, for it increases the available options in terms of trajectory.

There is some debate about the relative suitability of a lob wedge for golfers of different playing ability. Many tour pros favor a lob wedge with 60 degrees of loft because they know they will hit the ball a certain distance—and never more than that distance—on a high trajectory time after time. They can also use a lob wedge to execute "flop shots" that carry only a few yards on extremely high

trajectories. But many teaching pros advise average golfers not to carry a lob wedge because they are not as strong as tour pros and cannot achieve much distance with such a high-lofted club; also, average golfers are often tempted to try specialty shots like flop shots that are beyond their capabilities. Among the notable exceptions is Pelz, who advises both pro and amateur students alike to carry four wedges, for reasons that will be detailed below.

Along with loft, the main consideration to keep in mind when selecting your set of short-game tools is their design characteristics. Every club in your bag, including your wedges, has a "leading edge,"

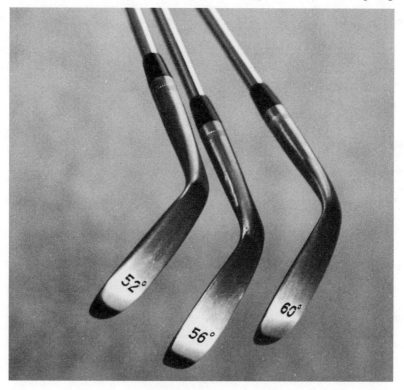

Wedges with Lofts of 52°, 56°, and 60°

which is the lower ridge on the front of the face, and a "flange," which is the mass of metal that protrudes from the rear of the face. The amount of slope between the leading edge and the trailing edge of the flange measured in degrees is called "bounce." Six degrees of bounce is moderate; 12 degrees is high.

Generally speaking, it is easier to hit shots from the fairway using clubs with relatively little bounce because they more readily allow the leading edge to cut through the grass. It is easier to hit bunker shots using clubs with more bounce because the bounce is what enables the club to slide through the sand underneath the ball; if you dig in with the leading edge, you're likely either to contact the ball before you contact the sand and hit the ball over the green, or take too much sand and leave the ball in the bunker.

For these reasons, virtually all the top teaching pros agree that you should assemble a set of wedges that have a variety of bounces as well as a variety of lofts. But there is considerable disagreement about the best methods for using these essential tools of the short game.

Unified-Swing Short-Game Methods

Most of the top-ranked teaching pros advocate a "unified-swing" approach to the short game. Their shared belief is that short-game shots should be played with only slightly modified variations on full swings or putting strokes. The differences between them mostly boil

down to whether they favor small-muscle, big-muscle, or mixed-muscle methods, or biomechanically based swing techniques.

You can get a quick overview of the similarities and differences between the unified-swing approaches to the short game by examining the pitching, chipping, and bunker shot techniques recommended by Jim Flick, who advocates small-muscle methods; Jim McLean, who advocates big-muscle methods; Butch Harmon, who advocates mixed-muscle methods; and Mike Adams, who advocates the LAWs of Golf method.

Small-muscle pitch shots. Jim Flick's method for executing a pitch shot is a miniature version of the small-muscle method he recommends for full shots, blended with a bit of putting technique. As in the full swing, he emphasizes the role of the hands and arms as the primary sources of touch and feel, insisting that the shoulders and body "simply don't have the sensitivity to control the angle and speed of the clubhead on short game shots."

In his "Eight Basics" for the standard pitch shot outlined in *On Golf: Lessons from America's Master Teacher,* Flick recommends positioning the ball in the middle of your stance, directly underneath your sternum, so that your right eye sees the back of the ball and your left eye sees the top of the ball. He believes pitch shots should be made with a "pendulum-like stroke" similar to a putting stroke—powered mainly by the arms, with only "minimal wrist cock" result-

ing from the length of the swing and the weight of the clubhead. "Don't be concerned with the amount of follow-through," he advises. "With correct grip pressure and arm freedom, momentum will take care of it."

Big-muscle pitch shots. Jim McLean's method for executing a pitch shot also includes an early wrist cock and a corresponding amount of hand action, but he incorporates considerably more big-muscle body action than Flick. He recommends setting up to a standard pitch shot with the ball "about in the middle" of your stance (but certainly not back toward your right foot), and with 60 to 70 percent of your weight on your left side. Although there is no weight shift on the backswing, McLean believes that the body should turn and shift as you swing your wedge though impact. "Think about keeping the club shaft centered on your body through impact and at the finish," he says. "Feel that your right hip or right pocket is turning past the ball."

In contrast to Flick, McLean pays considerable attention to controlling the length and height of both the backswing and the follow-through. On a short pitch of less than thirty yards, he recommends a high backswing and a low follow-through rather than a short backswing and a high follow-through. He is fond of quoting the "hit and resist" dictum of the late teaching pro Johnny Revolta. "Swing the club down through the ball and then resist at the finish," McLean advises, adding that you should keep your left

Setting Up for a Pitch Shot

wrist flat, especially on short pitches. Like his counterparts, he warns against trying to "scoop" or "flip" the ball into the air, noting that the loft of the wedge will do the work for you if you let it.

On long and intermediate pitch shots, McLean instructs students to make their backswings match their follow-throughs. His

recommended means for controlling distance is to calibrate your pitching motions according to positions on an imaginary clock face. When making a one-quarter-length pitch, you swing the clubhead back to four o'clock and swing it through to eight o'clock. A half swing goes back to nine o'clock through to three o'clock, a three-quarter swing goes back to ten o'clock and through to two o'clock, and a full swing goes back to eleven o'clock and through to one o'clock.

Mixed-muscle pitches. Butch Harmon's mixed-muscle method for executing pitch shots incorporates elements of both the Flick method and the McLean method, but with a special emphasis on feel as opposed to calibrating formulas. He advises students to position the ball "in the middle of your stance or maybe a ball width ahead of center," warning that many amateurs play the ball too far back in their stances and try to hit down too sharply. Like McLean, he believes you should set up for a standard pitch shot with more weight on your left side than your right side, but he also believes you should maintain a slightly open body alignment to enable you "to put a trace of out-to-in cut spin" on the shot.

Harmon recommends starting the backswing with a one-piece takeaway, keeping your wrists firm all the way to the top, and then starting the downswing with a body move to your left side. But unlike McLean, he advises against calibrating your backswing and follow-through according to an imaginary clock face. "Simply feel

how much swing you need for the distance, " he suggests. He also insists that there is no need to make more than a three-quarter-length swing on any pitch shot. "This shot is really all about the precise delivery of the clubhead through the ball," he says. "If you think a certain pitch is just out of your range with a sand iron and a three-quarter swing, use a pitching wedge."

Small-muscle chips. Flick's small-muscle method for executing chip shots is based on a principle that is also revered by advocates of big-muscle and mixed-muscle methods—i.e., "the less air time, the better." The shared premise here is that generally speaking, high-lofted shots are high-risk shots, while low-running shots are low-risk shots. That being the case, there is even more of a premium on club selection in chipping than there is in pitching, according to Flick. He advises students to select a club with just enough loft to carry the ball onto the green about three feet beyond the apron; the most likely choices, he says, are a six, seven, eight, or nine iron.

On most chip shots, Flick recommends positioning the ball toward the back of your stance, just to the right of your sternum. The worse the lie, he adds, the farther back you should position the ball. In contrast to a pitch, where your hands remain even with the ball at address and through impact, Flick says you should keep your hands ahead of the ball at all times on a chip shot, while maintaining slightly more grip pressure than on other shots. He believes

that you should make a "pendulum-like stroke" powered exclusively by your arms and shoulders, with the hands and wrists merely reacting to the weight of the clubhead, and that you should strike the ball on a descending arc created as a consequence of the back-in-the-stance ball position at address. "Don't be concerned with the amount of follow-through," he says, noting that the ground itself often stops the club shortly after impact.

Big-muscle chips. McLean's and Flick's methods for executing a chip shot are much closer to each other than are their respective pitching methods. McLean, too, advocates "minimum air time, maximum ground time," more grip pressure than on other shots, and a pendulum-like motion that is similar to a putting stroke. But he parts company with Flick on two points. First, he says that you should position the ball closer to your body with your eyes over the ball, as in a putt, and that you should arch your wrists slightly so that the shaft of the club is in a more upright position at address than on a standard pitch shot. Secondly, he believes that you should use at least some hip turn on longer chips to power the stroke.

Mixed-muscle chips. Harmon's method for executing a chip shot incorporates many of the same fundamentals as the Flick and McLean methods. He wants you to position the ball inside your right foot, with most of your weight on your left side. He wants you to keep your hands ahead of the ball at address and through impact.

3 Wood Chip Shot

And he wants you to keep your wrists relatively firm throughout the shot. But as in his pitching method, Harmon distinguishes himself from his peers in underscoring the importance of developing feel for chip shots rather than relying on any club selection formulas, a point he dramatizes in short-game drills on a special practice hole at the Butch Harmon School of Golf outside Las Vegas.

"All of the greens and the chipping areas surrounding them are sort of like human faces, with individual features and contours that are theirs and theirs alone," Harmon notes. "You just can't boil your chipping game down to a formula. Instead, practice your chipping from different lies, from different angles to different pin positions. Get a feel for the clubs that give you the best results." In that regard, Harmon has encouraged his star pupil Tiger Woods and other students to become proficient at using a three wood around the green, employing the same basic methodology he recommends for chip shots with other clubs.

Bunker shots. Bunker play is one area of the game where small-muscle, big-muscle, and mixed-muscle methods tend to converge. That's because most teaching pros who ascribe to a unified-swing approach advise that you power a standard bunker shot primarily with your hands and arms, and that you follow many of the same basic rules of setup and contact point to get a ball out of the sand. Likewise, virtually all of the top-ranked teaching pros try to alleviate their amateur students' deep-seated but irrational fear of executing a

bunker shot by reminding them that it is the most forgiving shot in golf because it is the one shot in which you do not have to make contact with the ball.

Flick urges his students to use essentially the same swing on sand shots that they use on regular full shots. The principal adjustments are in the setup. Like most of his peers, he emphasizes the importance of opening the face of your sand wedge at address, keeping your hands behind the ball, lowering your feet into the sand, and putting most of your weight on your left side. All of these pointers are intended to help you contact the sand on a descending arc, with the sloping portion of the flange that forms the bounce of the wedge rather than the leading edge. He calls the leading edge the "digger," and the bounce portion the "skimmer."

Flick believes the secret to successfully executing a standard bunker shot is to skim or scoop "a large cupful of sand" out of the bunker, letting the ball ride out on the sand. He contends that the best way for most amateurs students to accomplish this is by making a long, slow-tempo swing in which the club travels to at least the ten o'clock position on the backswing and then on to at least the two o'clock position on the follow-through.

Like other top teaching pros, Flick warns that digging into the sand with the leading edge of the wedge is a recipe for disaster. But so long as the flange or bounce of your club enters the sand first, he maintains, the contact point can be anywhere from two inches to five inches

behind the ball. "Trying to be too precise causes tension," he says, "and tension can tie you up." Where he differs from many of his peers, however, is in recommending that you position the ball in the center of your stance, directly under your sternum. According to Flick, if you position the ball forward of your sternum, the club will bottom out too far behind the ball, causing you to dig into the sand on your downswing or skull (that is, hit the top of the ball) on your through swing.

The bunker shot techniques recommended by McLean and Harmon are quite similar to each other, which is hardly surprising, as both men were tutored by Butch's late father, Claude Harmon Sr. Where Flick recommends using "lots of arm" on a bunker shot, McLean recommends that you make a full shoulder turn on your backswing in the interest of "building easy speed." By contrast, Harmon believes that for a right-handed player, "the sand shot is executed almost entirely by the right hand." In keeping with the teaching of Claude Sr., both McLean and Harmon advocate starting the downswing in big-muscle fashion with a forward bump of the lower body and then fully releasing the right hand through the shot in small-muscle fashion with what Harmon describes as "a hard slicing motion."

One subtle but significant difference between the bunker shot method advocated by McLean and Harmon and the method advocated by Flick involves the issue of ball position. Both McLean and Harmon recommend playing the ball well forward in your stance

Setting Up for a Bunker Shot

rather than in the center. They believe that a forward ball position makes it easier for you to slide your wedge through the sand underneath the ball, and that it is far better to enter the sand a little too far behind the ball because you can still get it out of the bunker and onto the green provided you do not decelerate on your downswing. If you enter the sand too close to the ball, they warn, you're in danger of skulling the ball over the green.

LAWs of Golf short-game techniques. The LAWs of Golf techniques for short-game shots developed by Mike Adams and his associates represent the most unified of the unified-swing approaches. The recommended takeaway on pitches, chips, and bunker shots is essentially the same as the takeaway a leverage player makes on a full swing (see chapter 3). The hands and arms control the motion leading to an early wrist cock, while the body remains relatively passive.

The major difference between the LAWs techniques and other methods is the prescribed means for controlling distances. Adams and his associates believe that the easiest and most efficient way to calibrate pitch shots and chip shots is through adjustments in setup, rather than by calibrating your backswing according to positions on a clock face. The principal setup adjustments involve three positions in three areas—your grip, your stance width, and your foot alignment.

On a full-length pitch, you are advised to hold your wedge at the end of the grip, as on a full swing with other clubs, to spread your heels about shoulder width apart, and to keep the toes of both

feet on a line parallel to your target line. On an intermediate pitch, you are advised to grip down halfway, to spread your heels about hip width apart, and to move your left foot back so the toes are even with the instep of your right foot. On a short pitch or chip, you are advised to grip even farther down, to narrow your stance inside hip width, and to align the toes of your left foot with your right heel.

Adams and his associates maintain that you can learn to calibrate the distances of your pitches in increments ranging from ten yards to five yards and less merely by experimenting with variations in grip, stance, and foot alignment similar to those described above. But they also caution that it is crucial to allow your chosen setup positions to govern the length of your swing. If you try to make a full swing with a choked-down grip and a narrow stance, for example, you'll likely lose balance and either hit the top of the ball or hit the turf behind the ball, thereby defeating your purpose.

The LAWs system for bunker play is based on three catchwords: face, base, and pace. Like his peers, Adams recommends that you set up for a standard bunker shot by making sure that you open the face of your sand wedge. The next step is to establish a stable base by digging in your feet into the sand; the shorter the bunker shot, the deeper you are advised to dig in. Finally, Adams urges his students to maintain a brisk and even tempo throughout their backswings and follow-throughs; he warns that any attempt to add pace (accelerate) or decrease pace (decelerate), especially during the

downswing, will destroy any chance of executing your bunker shots in a consistent and effective manner.

Multiple-Swing Short-Game Methods

The leading advocate of multiple-swing short-game methods is Dave Pelz. His approach is based on the belief that golf is not one game but five games: the power game, the putting game, the short game, the course management game, and the mental game. "Your short game is not like any of golf's other games," he declares in the opening pages of *Dave Pelz's Short Game Bible.* "It should not be played as if it's a throttled down version of the power game."

Where advocates of the unified-swing approach believe that you should use the same basic swing on full shots and short-game shots, Pelz contends that you need three swings to play your best golf. In his methodology, swing number one is the full swing you use in your power game, which he describes as a "hit" motion. Swing number two is the swing you use with your putter, which he describes as a "stroke" motion. Swing number three is for your short game, and he labels it a "finesse swing."

Pelz developed his unique approach to the short game over the past two decades with the help of several PGA Tour pros, including Tom Jenkins and Tom Kite, both of whom now compete on the Senior PGA Tour. He says his research showed that the

pros encountered diametrically opposite difficulties in controlling distance and direction on full shots and on short-game shots. On full swings with long and middle irons, the pros were generally good at controlling the distance of their shots but poor at controlling the direction. But on shots within 100 yards of the green, the pros were good at controlling direction but very poor at controlling distance.

The "finesse swing" was born of the efforts of Pelz and his PGA Tour protégés to control distances on wedge shots. It is a kind of mixed-muscle hybrid of a full swing and a putting stroke that relies on the big muscles for power and the small muscles for touch. Pelz claims that the finesse swing can be used on pitch shots, chip shots, and bunker shots alike with prescribed modifications in set up and ball position.

One of the goals of the finesse swing is to take the "hit" out of short-game shots to promote consistency, especially under tournament pressure. To that end, Pelz developed the concepts of "dead hands," his term for keeping the small muscles of the hands, wrists, fingers, and forearms passive throughout the swing, and the "synchronized turn," his term for rotating the big muscles of the upper body and lower body at the same speed from start to finish. The takeaway of the finesse swing is similar to the takeaway of a full swing, but when your hips stop turning on the backswing, your shoulders, hands, and arms also stop turning so that you don't cre-

ate any coil. On the downswing, your weight transfers to your left side, and your hips and forearms rotate through the shot.

Pelz further refined the finesse swing with a system for controlling distances by calibrating the length of the backswing and the follow-through according to five positions which also correspond to clock-face positions. In contrast to teaching pros like McLean who advocate balanced or equal length backswings and follow-throughs on most short-game shots, Pelz believes that the best way to make an accelerating swing is to "make a short backswing and a longer follow-through." On a three-quarter pitch shot, for example, he recommends a 3 backswing, which corresponds to the nine o'clock position on a clock face, and a full-length or 5 follow-through. But on a fifteen-yard pitch, which requires only a 1 backswing, he also recommends a 5 follow-through.

Unlike most of his peers in the teaching profession who caution that pulling rather than simply swinging the club through impact on short-game shots causes mishits, Pelz maintains that you should promote acceleration by pulling the club down, and that you should never push off from your back foot under any circumstances. He bases his advice on laws of physics that state that a mass that is pushed will rotate off line unless the pushing force remains directed precisely through the center, while a mass that is pulled will automatically align with and follow the pulling force. Translating all that into layman's terms, Pelz claims, "If a golfer continues

to accelerate and consistently pulls the club through impact, the club will continue to travel on a stable, repeatable path."

Pelz also departs from most of his peers on the issue of ball position for pitch shots, chip shots, and bunker shots. Where McLean says you should position the ball inside your right foot on a standard chip shot, Pelz says you should position the ball even farther back, opposite the ankle of your right foot. Where Harmon advises positioning the ball slightly forward of stance center on pitch shots, Pelz insists that the ball needs to be positioned in "the exact center" of your stance. And where Flick says you should position the ball in the center of your stance on a bunker shot, Pelz says you should position the ball much farther forward, inside your left heel.

Finally, Pelz is unique among his peers in advocating what he calls his "3x4 system" for distance control and club selection. Where many teaching pros, including Harmon, recommend that you carry three wedges with varying degrees of loft, he recommends that you carry four wedges—a pitching wedge, a sand wedge, a lob wedge, and an extra-lofted wedge. Pelz's reasoning is that with four wedges you can develop twelve shots of respectively consistent distances using three swings—a 10:30 swing, a 9:00 swing, and a 7:30 swing.

Picking Your "Perfect" Short-Game Method

The most important considerations in picking the short-game method that is "perfect" for you and your golfing goals are the amount of maintenance required, and the consistency and control you can achieve. In many ways, it boils down to a question of how well each method allows you to balance feel and calibrating formulas, mechanics and touch. For as short-game master Ray Floyd observes, "If you know the feel that works and can recapture it when you're playing, you won't have to worry about the ABCs, the mechanics, every time you step up to the ball. And you will be a much better player for it."

The unified-swing approaches are by and large more suited to average golfers than multiple-swing approaches. The advantages are continuity, simplicity, and relatively low maintenance. Generally speaking, you can execute pitch shots, chip shots, and even the standard bunker shot without having to learn or utilize a completely different set of techniques than those you use on longer shots. Practicing your short game will therefore help your full swing, and vice versa. And you can develop your touch without having to worry too much about mechanics.

The main disadvantage of the unified-swing approaches is that they are so simple, they may fail to offer sufficient precision and shot-

making options for some golfers. Several unified-swing approaches include calibrating formulas, but the primary emphasis is on feel. Although advocates cite this as an advantage, Pelz and the disciples of his multiple-swing approaches contend that relying so heavily on feel actually limits your ability to control distance and direction with consistency, and that your feel can and will desert you in the heat of competition. They also contend that just as you use different swings on full shots and on putts, you need a third specially customized swing to develop a first-class short game.

The Pelz multiple-swing approach is probably more suited to professionals and low-handicap amateurs who have the time and ability to develop new precision skills than to average golfers who have limited playing ability and limited practice time. The advantages are its potential for precision in distance control and variety in shot-making options. Pelz has literally broken the short game down into an almost exact science, with a backswing and a wedge loft to suit virtually any situation. The disadvantages are its inherent complexity and the fact that it is a high-maintenance system that requires you to learn and practice a finesse swing different from your full swing. Although you can develop a considerable amount of touch along the way, the multiple-swing approach requires you, at least initially, to pay quite a bit of attention to mechanics.

No matter which method you ultimately select, the three keys to learning how to improve your short game are the same.

1 Creativity. One of the things that makes golf such an endlessly fascinating game is the variety of lies and shot-making options a player can face within 100 yards of the green. Remember that a method is merely the means to an end, and the goal of your short game is to get the ball as close to the hole as possible, if not in the hole. Here more than in any other area of the game it really isn't how you accomplish that end but how many strokes you take to do it. Experiment with the standard methods as much as you like, but also try whenever possible to invent shots of your own. The short game is where you can really "play" golf in the fullest and most creative sense of the word.

2 Practice. That sounds simple and obvious, but it's something that most amateurs neglect, to their ultimate regret. Improving your short game is the best and fastest way to improve your scores and lower your handicap. Practicing the short game will remain vitally important to improving your scoring, no matter how good you get in other aspects of the game. As noted above, even the pros hit only about 65 percent of the greens on average.

3 More practice. Once you've mastered the basics of your chosen method, keep refining them until they become second nature. Remember, as Butch Harmon points out, for the pros "practicing the short game is almost a religion." If you really want to play better golf, make practicing the short game your religion, too.

SUMMARY: *Top Teaching Pros and Their Short-Game Methods*

▶ UNIFIED-SWING APPROACHES

Advocates of unified-swing approaches maintain that short-game shots should be played with miniature versions of a full swing or a putting stroke. Several offer formulas for calibrating distances by backswing length or adjustments in setup, but the primary emphasis is on feel. The fact that the same basic techniques are used on full swings and short-game shots may make unified-swing approaches easier for average golfers to learn and practice.

Small-Muscle Method

Jim Flick, Bob Toski

Big-Muscle Method

Jimmy Ballard, Michael Hebron, David Leadbetter, Jim McLean

Mixed-Muscle Method

Chuck Cook, Hank Haney, Butch Harmon, Rick Smith

LAWs of Golf Technique

Mike Adams, Dr. Jim Suttie, T. J. Tomasi

▶MULTIPLE-SWING APPROACHES

The pioneer and leading advocate of multiple-swing approaches to the short game is Dave Pelz. He maintains that the short game is so important, it demands a customized "finesse swing" that is different from a full swing and a putting stroke. The primary emphasis is on precision in distance control through calibrating formulas and the use of four wedges. The relative complexity and new skill learning required by Pelz's system may make it more suitable for pros and top amateurs than average golfers.

Dave Pelz

5 GOLF YOUR BALL:
Minding and Managing Your Game

Call me the Yogi Berra of golf, but I firmly believe that 50 percent of the game is mental, and so is the other half. If you want to realize your full potential as a golfer, you need more than a sound putting stroke, a fluid full swing, and a deadly accurate short game. You also need to master the strategic, psychological, and emotional aspects of golf. As Bobby Jones observed in his instructional manual *Bobby Jones On Golf,* "A good part of the game is played between the ears; meaning that judgment, based on thought and experience, is often as important as mechanical skill."

Jones knew what he was talking about from personal experience, similar to, if far more storied than, my own humbling mental bumbling. In his teenage years, he demonstrated remarkable mechanical skill that belied his age. But he had to improve his judgment and conquer an adolescent anger problem that culminated in a scorecard-tearing tantrum on the Old Course at St. Andrews before he could attain the golfing proficiency required to win the

Grand Slam. Along with Jones, three other great champions stand out as masters of the part of the game that is played between the ears. They are Walter Hagen, Jack Nicklaus, and Tiger Woods.

Often depicted in the press as a champagne-swilling bon vivant, Hagen won eleven major championships between 1914 and 1927. His seemingly carefree attitude was what enabled him to focus on the competition at hand without any noticeable trace of mental or physical tension, the bogeymen of consistently first-class golf. "I've never played a perfect eighteen holes," Hagen once said. "There is no such thing. I expect to make at least seven mistakes a round. Therefore, when I make a bad shot, I don't worry about it. It's just one of the seven."

The young Jack Nicklaus was marveled at by his peers even more for his extraordinary mental prowess than for the extraordinary distances he hit the ball off the tee. The Golden Bear won twenty major championships by demonstrating unrivaled strategic thinking in navigating his way around the world's toughest golf courses, and by using pre-shot visualization techniques he called "going to the movies."

Tiger Woods is the heir apparent to Nicklaus as the greatest golfer who ever played the game. Woods is renowned for his athleticism and his fist-pumping flair for drama. But notwithstanding a few isolated outbursts now and again, he has emulated Jones in channeling a fiery temper into a Zen-like focus that has him on track to win more majors than any golfer in history.

As the careers of all four of these golfing greats attest, the part of the game that is played between the ears is actually two games— the **course management game** and the **emotional management game.** These two games are distinct and at the same time insepara- ble. They are also inextricably intertwined with the physical side of golf, and with the ultimate aim of the game itself, which is to play the course at hand in the lowest possible number of strokes.

You don't have to be Sigmund Freud to recognize how the course management and emotional management styles of golfers at all levels mirror the way golf courses are designed. The three leading schools of golf course architecture are the penal style, which rewards good shots and severely punishes bad ones; the heroic style, which encourages the weighing of risk and reward in shot making; and the strategic style, which places a premium on strategy in shot placement. Likewise, and not just coincidentally, the ways most golfers manage their emotions and the courses they play can be described as penal, heroic, strategic, or some combina- tion of the three.

The majority of average golfers tend to the penal with quixotic and usually ill-fated touches of the heroic. They set themselves up for defeat by making poor course management decisions or by attempting shots beyond their capabilities; then they punish them- selves emotionally when their shots end up in trouble. Most profes- sionals try to balance the strategic and the heroic. They generally

make sound strategic course management decisions and take heroic risks only when their skills promise a reasonable chance of reward; when shots go awry, they either punish themselves quickly and get it over with, or they try to maintain an even emotional keel following both bad shots and good ones.

There is an ongoing debate among great golfers and great golf instructors over the relative importance of course management and emotional management vis à vis the physical aspects of the game. Nicklaus, for example, believes that golf is 50 percent mental, 40 percent setup, and 10 percent swing. Jim McLean and Butch Harmon take issue with that formulation. McLean's "25 percent theory" holds that the full swing, the short game (including putting), the course management game, and the emotional game merit equal weight. Harmon's "four cornerstones" consist of the full swing, the short game, the management/mental game, and physical fitness.

Despite the nitpicking over percentages, virtually all top players and top teaching pros agree that learning how to manage the course and learning how to manage your emotions are essential to learning how to improve your game. Why? Because mastering those two skills is what makes it possible for you to relax and actually play golf when you go out on the course—and to have fun doing it.

Course Management Techniques

Course management means different things to different golfers and different golf instructors. And as noted above, it is closely tied to management of your emotions, as well as to the physical aspects of the game. For our purposes, course management can be defined as those mental skills pertaining to the information-gathering and decision-making processes and ritual behavior required to play each shot and each hole on a golf course.

With only minor exceptions, the course management techniques prescribed by the game's top teaching pros are far more similar in form and in substance than their putting, short-game, and full-swing techniques. It makes no difference whether you prefer to hit the ball with small-muscle, big-muscle, or mixed-muscle methods, or whether you prefer to putt with an arc stroke or a pendulum stroke. You are always playing against the same two opponents—the golf course and yourself.

The first point on which all the top teaching pros concur is the importance of distinguishing between practicing golf and playing golf. You practice golf on the practice range, on the putting green, or in front of a mirror or video camera. Those are the places where you learn and refine your techniques. When you step out on the golf course, you must quit practicing and start to play the game. Here again, Bobby Jones put it in straight and simple terms. "Once the

round is underway, the business in hand becomes that of getting results," he declared in *On Golf*. "Nothing else matters."

Among other things, playing golf means focusing on "the business in hand"—that is, getting the ball into the hole in the fewest strokes possible. It does not mean focusing on mechanics, tinkering with your swing, or trying to correct your technique after every wayward shot. When you're out on the golf course, you should not be concerned with the art of ball striking, the art of putting, or the art of the short game. Your sole concern should be the art of scoring. And the art of scoring is not about practicing golf, it's about playing golf.

The second point on which all the top teachers concur is that you need to do a significant amount of information gathering before and during each round in order to manage the course to the best of your ability. Specifically, you have to know the course, know the playing conditions, know your distances for each club in your bag, and know your own physical and mental condition.

"Good course managers plot their course starting at the hole and working back to the tee," Butch Harmon observes in *Four Cornerstones of Winning Golf*. Sound familiar? It should. That is the same prescription Harvey Penick offered for learning the fundamentals of shot making, and it makes good strategic sense, as well. By starting at the hole and working backward, you can determine the angle from which it is best to approach a certain pin. If, for example, you're playing a dogleg left par four where there is a

bunker guarding the left side of the green and the pin is on the left half of the green, the best approach angle is likely to be from the right. That automatically tells you that there is little to be gained from trying to cut the dogleg with a big draw off the tee; instead, it makes more sense to position your drive on the right side of the fairway to set up a clear approach, even if it leaves you with a slightly longer shot.

Knowing the playing conditions is equally crucial to the art of scoring. If the course has been rained on the night before, for example, the fairways are likely to be soft, and your drives will not roll as far as they would if the fairways were dry. At the same time, the greens are also likely to be soft, so they'll probably hold your approach shots, which in turn indicates that you can land the ball closer to the pin than you might otherwise be able to do. Knowing the playing conditions means accounting for such variables as the strength and direction of the wind, the temperature (when it's below 50 degrees, the ball will not carry as far), and even the length and thickness of the grasses in the fairways and the roughs.

You can further improve your ability to score by doing some preround information gathering about yourself. How far do you hit with each club in your bag under normal conditions? Most pros know the distances they carry the ball with their woods and irons within a couple of yards at most. Most average golfers, on the other hand, have only a vague idea that varies up to as much as ten yards

per club. That's not precise enough. Ten yards translates into thirty feet when you're on the green. When gauging distances for their clubs, the pros are also aware of their own physical and mental condition on the day in question. Are you feeling strong and flexible? Or are you a little stiff and tired? The answers to those questions will have a significant impact on your ball striking.

The third point the top teaching pros agree on is that the best way to get results in terms of course management is to learn to think strategically. Thinking strategically entails planning your approach to the round as a whole, planning your approach to each hole, and planning your approach to each shot. Sound strategic thinking is based in part on the information gathering you do before the round as outlined above, but it also incorporates the information gathering you do during the round, including accounting for changing conditions out on the course, and a realistic assessment of your own golfing capabilities.

The key to effective course management in general and strategic thinking in particular is to play your own game. Amateur golfers are best advised to strategize according to their handicap level. An eighteen handicapper, for example, should try to play "bogey golf" from tee to green on each hole. Trying to reach every par four hole in two shots that are probably beyond your present capabilities often leads to double bogeys or worse. It makes more sense to devise a strategy that enables you to reach the green of a par four in three

shots that you are easily capable of making. You'll still allow yourself the chance to make a one-putt par, you'll avoid costly double bogeys, you'll put less strain on your game, and you'll have more fun.

If you're a short hitter who happens to be paired with a long ball hitter, don't allow yourself to get sucked into a driving contest. Playing golf isn't about how far you hit the ball, it's about the art of scoring. Always swing within yourself. As Jim McLean advises, "leave your ego in the bag." It doesn't matter if your playing partner can hit a seven iron to a par three hole and you need to hit a five iron. What matters is getting your ball in the hole in the fewest possible strokes.

Play to your strengths and away from your weaknesses. Pick specific targets off the tee, but don't get greedy. Play the percentages, judiciously weighing risk and reward. You don't always have to try to cut the corner of a dogleg or aim for a small landing area, even if it offers the best approach angle. Putting your drive in the middle of the fairway is almost always far better than leaving it in the rough. If you tend to fade or slice the ball, aim to the left and let your natural shot bring the ball back toward the target. Don't try to make swing changes that will enable you to hit draws or hooks while you're out on the course. Be wise and flexible in your club selection. Don't automatically pull out your driver on every par four or par five hole if a three wood or long iron can put you in the fairway and set up approach shots of reasonable lengths.

If you hit an errant tee shot into the rough, don't automatically assume that you've got to go for the green on your second shot to have any chance of saving par. That kind of thinking often leads average golfers to wind up making double bogeys or worse. They either choose a club without enough loft to get the ball out of the rough, or they follow their errant drives with an errant approach into a bunker or water hazard. One good way to avoid such a predicament is to follow what McLean calls the "divide by two rule." Let's say a poor tee shot has left you 260 yards from the green. Even if you bust a three wood, you're not likely to reach the putting surface. Instead, simply divide the distance by two, and you've got two shots of 130 yards that you can comfortably execute with a short iron.

The fourth point all the top teaching pros agree on is the importance of developing and faithfully executing a sound pre-shot routine. A pre-shot routine is basically a ritual that you perform the same way every time before you hit the ball. It is what allows you to block out mechanical thoughts so that you keep your attention on the task at hand. It is what allows you to focus on the process of playing in the present tense rather than worrying about some future result. In other words, it is what allows you to focus exclusively on the art of scoring. By nature and definition, pre-shot routines vary from golfer to golfer, but the routines recommended by most top teaching pros incorporate the following elements:

First pick a specific target, then visualize the shot you want to hit

and the swing you need to make that shot. This visualization process is what Nicklaus called "going to the movies." Next, make a "rehearsal swing." This is not a practice swing. It is a physical rehearsal of the kind of swing you've just visualized in your mind's eye. Most average golfers make haphazard or foreshortened rehearsal swings. Most PGA Tour pros make sure that their rehearsal swings are complete in form and smooth in tempo, matching the swing they want to put on the ball as closely as possible.

Once you've completed your rehearsal swing, it's time to address the ball, with your focus on your target and virtually nothing else. Many top players approach their address position from behind the ball; others approach from a ninety-degree angle. It doesn't matter which approach you take, so long as you take the same one every time.

The address portion of the pre-shot routine is when the minds of many average golfers are flooded with swing thoughts, most of which are crippling and unnecessary. Some top teaching pros believe you should have no swing thoughts at all; others maintain that having one or two good swing thoughts is better than having no swing thoughts. But none of the top teaching pros recommend having more than one swing thought for your backswing and one swing thought for your downswing.

What you should avoid at all costs is going through a mental checklist of several mechanical thoughts as you address the ball. That defeats the purpose of a pre-shot routine. Going through a

checklist tends to introduce unwanted physical and mental tension, and to cause you to forget about focusing on your target. If you must have swing thoughts, virtually all the top teaching pros urge that you keep them as simple and nonmechanical as you can. "Slow and easy back" is an example of what is considered a good swing thought. "Keep that right elbow tucked and keep your damn head down" is an example of what is considered a poor swing thought.

Your pre-shot routine must provide a cue for initiating your swing. Most of the top teaching pros recommend that you use a physical action to start your backswing. One such physical action is the waggle, which consists of hovering the club above the ground and gently rotating it a small circle for a specified number of times. But quite a few great players, including Jones, Hogan, and Nicklaus, have culminated their waggles with a forward press of their hands or their hips or their knees. Other great players have relied on a visual image or silent verbal cue. Again, it doesn't matter what you choose as a cue for initiating your swing. The important thing is that you incorporate something into your pre-shot routine that signals it's time to pull the trigger—and that you do the same thing every time without having to think about it.

Emotional Management Techniques

Knowing how to manage your emotions is every bit as essential to the art of scoring as knowing how to manage the golf course. The

two disciplines are so inextricably intertwined, both in general and in specific areas such as the pre-shot routine, that it is almost impossible to discuss course management without discussing emotional management and vice versa. For our purposes, emotional management can be defined as the mental skills required to effectively cope with the thoughts, feelings, and sensations you may experience before, during, and after a round of golf.

Until quite recently, many top golfers regarded emotional management and virtually all things psychological as taboo subjects. No self-respecting tour pro wanted even to mention a word like "choking," much less get involved in a public discussion of why he or some other player might have a tendency to perform at less than full potential under the pressure of competition. And while many pros might acknowledge the potential benefits of visualization techniques, given their use by the likes of Jack Nicklaus, few if any would admit to an interest in self-hypnosis or relaxation techniques.

All that is steadily changing, thanks in part to the demonstrated breakthroughs sports psychologists have achieved over the past two decades by prescribing emotional management programs for athletes in sports ranging from boxing and swimming to gymnastics and track and field. One of the best-known and most sought-after sports psychologists in golf is Dr. Bob Rotella, who has advised PGA Tour players like Lee Janzen, Davis Love III, Mark O'Meara, and Brad Faxon, as well as scores of amateur, college, and high

school players. Rotella's success in helping these golfers cope with competitive pressure, and his best-selling books *Golf Is Not a Game of Perfect, Golf Is a Game of Confidence,* and *The Golf of Your Dreams,* have helped remove much of the stigma previously attached to psychological counseling.

Of course, Rotella is neither the only nor, with all due respect, the most influential factor in the growing acceptance of sport psychology. New insights from clinical research into the functioning of the human mind and its relationship to peak performance, along with the ever-broadening dissemination of that information through the educational system and the media, have also helped debunk primitive myths and misconceptions.

One of those myths is that the anxiety you feel under stress or competitive pressure—and associated symptoms such as sweaty palms, a pounding heart, or the shortness of breath labeled "choking"—is all in your head. Anxiety experienced under stress or competitive pressure is not all in your head, a fact that is especially important for golfers to understand. Anxiety is a physical as well as psychological phenomenon, and its roots can be traced to the "fight or flight" syndrome that has both helped and hobbled the human race since the dawn of history.

In situations involving threat and stress, the human nervous system secretes a variety of extremely powerful chemicals. They include relatively well known substances such as adrenaline and

somewhat lesser known ones such as norepinephrine. As Dr. James E. Loehr and Peter J. McLaughlin point out in *Mentally Tough: The Principles of Winning at Sports Applied to Winning in Business,* norepinephrine can have the effect of dilating your pupils, making your eyes more sensitive to their surroundings, and increasing your pulse, which brings more blood (and more energy) to your muscles.

Back in ancient times, chemicals like norepinephrine were an integral part of the human survival mechanism. They enhanced our ability either to fight the force that threatened us or to take flight from it. In modern times, however, they can wreak havoc with all forms of human endeavor. Nowhere is this more evident than in a sport like golf.

In golf, we encounter perceived threats and experience fear at every turn. There is the fear of hitting over water. There is the fear of bunkers, trees, rough, and hardpan lies. There is the fear of embarrassing yourself in front of playing partners or in front of a gallery. There is the fear of failure, the fear of not making a cut in an important tournament, the fear of letting down a partner and/or yourself by failing to play up to your potential. There is even the fear of success that rears its ugly head when you play better than expected in the early going, then slam on the brakes and start playing poorly until you get back into a familiar "comfort zone."

These are the types of situations that prompt the onslaught of anxiety-producing chemicals. They destroy your swing tempo,

cloud your judgment, and give you all manner of emotional fits ranging from fear and loathing to club-hurling outrage and anger, whether you're competing in a major championship, trying to win a two-dollar nassau with your Saturday-morning foursome, or simply trying to break 100 for the first time. Average golfers experience their ill effects as much if not more than the pros. As the golfing psychiatrist Dr. Phil Lee and teaching pro Jeff Warne point out in their emotional management guide *Shrink Your Handicap,* anxiety-producing chemicals are what transform the often relaxed and respectable game you play on the practice range into the nightmarish version you play out on the course.

The bad news is that there is no way you can shut off or completely eliminate the functions of the human nervous system associated with the primordial fight-or-flight reflex without resorting to medication. (In fact, some pros have used drugs called beta blockers, typically prescribed for people with heart problems. But, in addition to calming you down, they can also make you feel lethargic.) The good news is that you can call on a wide variety of techniques to help defend yourself against anxiety-producing chemicals and cope with the stress of competitive pressure, ranging from psychological to physical to metaphysical approaches.

Just as teaching pros can be categorized according to the types of swing theories they advocate, experts in the field of emotional management can be divided into two major schools. Some mental

coaches, like Rotella, have what might be described as a unitary methodology, preferring to focus only on one or two approaches they believe to be applicable to most of their clients. Lee is a pioneer of what might be described as a multidisciplinary methodology. Applying the same basic insights about the effects of anxiety-producing chemicals on golfers that Loehr and his colleagues have used in their work with tennis players, Lee uses four different approaches, encouraging clients to choose the approach or combination of approaches best suited to their individual personalities.

Here are some of the major approaches and specific techniques recommended by Rotella, Lee, and other experts:

Cognitive approaches. The goals of cognitive defenses against anxiety are to correct illogical thoughts that leap into your mind under competitive pressure and to replace them with logical thoughts that will improve your chances of shooting a good score. This is one of the approaches advocated by Rotella, as well as by Lee. It is also the approach Walter Hagen used when he told himself not to worry about hitting one bad shot because he expected to hit at least seven bad shots in any given round. If you're an average golfer, you may expect to hit more than seven bad shots in eighteen holes, but the point is not to attach special significance to any one of them. Let's say you hit a bad tee shot on the first hole. There is no reason to conclude that you will therefore hit a bad tee shot on the remaining seventeen holes. After

all, every tee shot on every hole is separate and distinct from every other tee shot on every other hole. The cognitive approach would be to replace an illogical thought like, "I hit a bad tee shot on the first hole, so I'm going to hit bad tee shots all day," with a logical thought like, "Although I got off to a bad start, I still have a chance to play well on the holes ahead."

The advantages of cognitive approaches are that they are simple, straightforward, and require no special training. Most golfers know how to think in a logical manner. The problem is, that's often much easier said than done. The disadvantage of cognitive techniques is that they depend on willpower and the power of positive thinking. Like his philosophical mentor William James, Rotella believes strongly in the concept of "free will." The question is, do you, and if so, how well are you able to exercise your free will amid the onslaught of anxiety-producing chemicals?

Insight-oriented approaches. The goal of insight-oriented approaches is to resolve past conflicts that are crippling your game in the present. This approach is in many ways the exact opposite of the cognitive approach, and it often involves some form of psychoanalysis. A classic example is a golfer who plays what Lee and Warne call "the blame game" after hitting a bad shot. His mental processes might go as follows: "There I go hitting another bad shot. That means I'm a bad person."

Telling yourself you hit a bad shot because you're a bad person

is illogical, to be sure, but it may occur for reasons that have a logic of their own related to larger psychological and emotional issues. The blame game may originate in childhood conflicts with your parents or with an older sibling, during which you learned to blame yourself as a way of avoiding even more severe reprisals. If that's the case, the insight-oriented approach maintains that you need to resolve your parental conflicts or your sibling rivalry first, so you can stop playing the blame game and start playing a good game of golf. Along the way, you must make what Lee and Warne call a "mental swing change" in which you replace blaming with curiosity about the causes of your bad shots.

The advantages of insight-oriented techniques are that they address what may be at the root of your emotional management difficulties, and that they do not depend solely on willpower or the power of positive thinking, both of which may be impossible for you to exercise if you're preoccupied with deep-seated parental conflicts. The disadvantage of insight-oriented techniques is that they may require you to seek help from a therapist, which can be expensive and time-consuming and involve a much more extensive self-examination than you thought you bargained for when you hit a few bad golf shots. On the other hand, that may be precisely what you need to get your game and your life together once and for all.

Behavioral approaches. The goal of behavioral approaches is to change the self-defeating ways you behave under stress or competi-

tive pressure by deliberately exposing you to the very things that strike fear into your heart. It is more or less equivalent to hopping back on the bicycle every time you fall off until you learn to ride it. Knowingly or unknowingly, beginning golfers actually engage in a form of behavior modification when they force themselves to keep going out on the course even though they may fear the immediate consequences. Over time, their fears should start to subside as they start to play better—and vice versa.

Experts in behavioral approaches report that you can overcome a fear of almost anything through exposure to the cause of your fear for a sustained sixty-minute period they refer to as the "magic hour." Given that you never stand over a full shot or even a putt for more than a few seconds, Lee has devised a technique to accelerate the process, the "headset drill," in which you listen to a taped cassette of negative thoughts ("He's going to slice it. . . . He's going to hit it in the water. . . .") for a sustained period equivalent to the magic hour. Eventually, you simply start to tune out these negative messages.

Among the advantages of behavioral approaches is that they take the bull by the horns without getting you sidetracked into convoluted psychoanalytic explanations. Unlike cognitive approaches, they do not offer a Pollyannaish dose of positive thinking. You simply confront your fears until they go away. The disadvantages of behavioral approaches are that you have to muster a certain modicum of

courage to make the required confrontation in the first place, and that you must keep summoning that courage long enough for the effects to take hold. The therapy may also require you to walk around the practice area and/or the golf course wearing a headset, which can be a pretty courageous act in and of itself.

Relaxation and self-hypnosis approaches. The goal of most relaxation and self-hypnosis approaches is to replace or bypass the negative mental images inspired by your fears with positive mental images associated with past or imagined situations characterized by physical relaxation, psychic calm, and a sense of well being. Relaxation and self-hypnosis have been used by Rotella in combination with his preferred cognitive approaches, and by other sports psychologists such as Lee in combination with insight-oriented approaches.

Relaxation and self-hypnosis techniques typically involve some form of meditation. You start by lying on a bed or sitting in a comfortable chair, closing your eyes, and taking a series of deep breaths. In a relaxation exercise, you focus on tightening and then relaxing various muscle groups, exhaling tension and inhaling relaxation. In a self-hypnosis exercise, you begin with similar muscle relaxation exercises accompanied by a verbal mantra ("My arm is getting heavy. . . . My legs are getting heavy") that segues into the conjuring of an image of a real or imagined place that is peaceful and secure. When you encounter stress or anxiety out on the golf course, you invoke a

kind of time-compressed version of the exercises you have performed at home by briefly closing your eyes and taking some deep breaths.

One of the advantages of relaxation and self-hypnosis approaches is that they address both the physical and the psychological elements of anxiety by simultaneously relaxing your body and your mind. They can also improve your sense of calm and well-being in other areas of your life besides golf. The disadvantages are that both approaches, like other forms of meditation, require a certain sustained discipline, and that you may have to practice the exercises over an extended period of time at home before you can easily invoke a foreshortened version of them when you're out on the golf course.

Metaphysical approaches. The goal of metaphysical approaches is to banish fear and anxiety to virtual oblivion by achieving a higher spiritual state that transcends both the physical and the psychological. Metaphysical approaches combine elements of insight-oriented approaches, cognitive approaches, and relaxation and self-hypnosis approaches, and to a lesser degree, elements of behavioral approaches. More of a holistic philosophy and outlook on life than a technique, they are most enthusiastically advocated in books such as Michael Murphy's *Golf in the Kingdom* and M. Scott Peck's *Golf and the Spirit: Lessons for the Journey.*

Metaphysical approaches see golf as a metaphor for life, and posit that both golf and life are merely parts of a much larger spiritual quest for enlightenment. As Murphy writes of his mythic Scottish golf pro Shivas Irons, "After the tournament he could see that golf

and his inner life were one destiny. He'd be a golf professional and a philosopher using the game to body forth the truths he was discovering within." Peck says essentially the same thing in more personal terms: "In doing battle on the golf course against my own personality—against my own ego, if you will—I am attempting to . . . [get] myself out of my own way. It is what spiritual growth is all about."

The advantages of metaphysical approaches are that they strike to the very core of your being, your spirit as well as your mind and body, and that they both elevate the game of golf and relegate it to its proper context as merely one part, albeit a compelling part, of your life's journey. The disadvantage of metaphysical approaches is that they can be hard to grasp and even harder to put to practical use without years of study and contemplation.

Physical techniques. Physical techniques for managing emotions fall into two categories according to their separate but related goals. One category of physical techniques aims to bypass mental demons by focusing your attention on familiar actions. Another category of physical techniques aims to condition your body in such a manner that you gain the overall health and confidence to confront your mental demons and perform at a peak level under competitive pressure.

Goal number one is addressed by physical techniques that involve rituals to be performed as part of your pre-shot routine. These rituals do not include making a forward press or waggling your club as you address the ball. Rather, they are similar to the idio-

syncratic gestures you typically see a baseball pitcher make as he prepares to step on the rubber. They include such things as tugging on the brim of your cap, hitching up your pants, or unfastening and refastening the Velcro on your golf glove before making a shot.

The advantage of ritual gestures is that they offer a simple and personalized means for overcoming fear and anxiety. When performed repeatedly in exactly the same manner, they give you a feeling of familiarity in uncertain situations and signal that it's okay for you to proceed. The disadvantage is that they may not be enough in and of themselves to stave off, much less exorcise, your inner demons.

Goal number two is addressed by physical fitness conditioning programs. If it seems odd to include physical fitness in a discussion of emotional management techniques, just take note of what Butch Harmon has to say on the subject. "I consider physical conditioning to be the fourth cornerstone of winning golf," he declares, "because it influences how you play every shot, and, I believe, how well you think about every shot." In other words, Harmon is basically restating and enthusiastically endorsing the ancient Greek concept of the connection between a sound mind and a sound body.

While it is beyond the scope of this book to describe and evaluate the leading physical conditioning programs for golfers, two points are worth noting. The first point is that most fitness experts agree a comprehensive physical conditioning program should include strengthening exercises for improving your muscular power and coordination;

stretching exercises for keeping your muscles loose and improving your flexibility; aerobic exercises such as running, bicycling, or jumping rope for your cardiovascular system; and a regimen for warming up before you practice or go out on the golf course.

Secondly, most fitness experts agree with Harmon that physical conditioning is one of the keys to learning how to improve your game. If you have any doubts about the otherwise obvious advantages of physical conditioning, you need only look to the performance levels Harmon's star pupil Tiger Woods has attained since embarking on a rigorous training program in 1997. Provided you do not suffer any medical or physical disabilities that preclude exercising (in which case you probably should not be playing golf), the disadvantages of physical conditioning are virtually nil.

Your Heart, Your Head, and Your Hands

"Play in the present." That is the universally accepted dictum prescribed by course management and emotional management experts of every stripe. Bobby Jones referred to it as tending to the business in hand, the art of shooting the best score you possibly can. To do that, you can't be fixated on what has happened in the past, good or bad, and you can't worry about or even look forward to what may happen in the future. You can only focus on what you have to accomplish in the present, and keep on trying regardless of what

happens, good or bad. Modern-day PGA Tour pros like Tiger Woods have a term for that. They call it "golfing your ball."

Course management is one set of basic mental skills every golfer needs to golf his ball and to be proficient at the art of scoring. The four points on which all the top teaching pros concur concerning course management are: (1) the importance of remembering that playing golf is different from practicing golf; (2) the importance of doing a significant information gathering before and during a round; (3) the importance of thinking strategically; and (4) the importance of developing and executing a consistent pre-shot routine.

Emotional management is a separate but closely related set of mental skills every golfer needs to golf his ball and to be proficient at the art of scoring. Among the methods recommended for helping you cope with the thoughts, feelings, and sensations you may experience before, during, or after a round are: cognitive techniques, insight-oriented techniques, behavioral techniques, relaxation and self-hypnosis techniques, metaphysical techniques, and physical techniques.

Allen Doyle maintains that in order to play first-class golf, you need to achieve proficiency in the use of what he calls "the three H's"—your heart, your head, and your hands. Doyle is hardly a household name like Bobby Jones or Tiger Woods, but he speaks from hard-won experience. A former college hockey player, he began to concentrate on golf relatively late in life and went on to

become an outstanding amateur player. By the time he reached his late forties, Doyle was operating a driving range in La Grange, Georgia, and he had two daughters approaching college age. In order to provide for his daughters' education, he turned pro and qualified for the PGA Tour at age forty-seven. He is now one of the stars of the Senior PGA Tour.

Not everyone can be Allen Doyle. In fact, most people lack the extraordinary talent and determination he has demonstrated over the past half decade. Be that as it may, everyone, including the average golfer, can work on their three H's. Your heart, which stands for the spiritual and emotional aspects of golf, provides you with a love for the game and the desire to improve. Your head, which stands for the strategic aspects of the game, provides you the brainpower to manage the course. Your hands stand for the physical aspects of the game, your ball striking, short game, and putting. As Doyle notes, you're likely to be stronger in one of the H's than the others, but you need proficiency in at least two H's to be a good player, and proficiency in all three to achieve your greatest potential.

The course management and emotional management techniques discussed in this chapter show you what are currently believed to be the most effective ways to use your heart, your head, and your hands. But regardless of which of them you choose, the only way you can truly improve your game is keep on playing the game, to keep on golfing your ball.

SUMMARY: *Minding and Managing Your Golf Game*

▶ COURSE MANAGEMENT

Course management is defined as those mental skills pertaining to the information-gathering, decision-making processes, and ritual behavior required to play each shot and each hole on a golf course. Top teaching pros concur on four key points:

1   **Always remember that playing golf is different from practicing golf.** Practicing golf is about learning and refining techniques. Playing golf is about the art of scoring.

2   **Do a significant amount of information gathering before and during a round.** You need to know the course, the playing conditions, the distances for each club in your bag, and your own physical and mental condition.

3   **Learn to think strategically.** Play your own game. Swing within yourself. Leave your ego in your bag. Play to your strengths and away from your weaknesses.

4   **Use a consistent pre-shot routine.** Go through the same ritual for taking aim, addressing the ball, and triggering your swing in the same manner and at the same pace every time you play a shot.

Emotional Management

Emotional management is defined as the mental skills required to effectively cope with the thoughts, feelings, and sensations you may experience before, during, and after a round of golf. The leading recommended techniques for defending against the onslaught of anxiety-producing chemicals are:

Cognitive: Correct illogical thoughts and replace them with logical thoughts.

Insight-oriented: Resolve past conflicts that hinder present performance.

Behavioral: Change behavior through exposure to stimuli of anxiety.

Relaxation and self-hypnosis: Conjure positive imagery through meditation.

Metaphysical: See golf and life as part of a spiritual journey.

Physical: Lessen anxiety through familiar actions and/or fitness conditioning.

6 ON LEARNING GOLF:
Seeking and Finding the Best Instruction

This chapter takes its title and inspiration from a book written by Percy Boomer over half a century ago. Boomer was a legendary teaching pro from Jersey off the coast of England, the same place where Harry Vardon was born, and his contributions to theories about how to swing a golf club and how to stroke a putt were far ahead of their time. In his book *On Learning Golf,* first published in 1946 and still in print, Boomer outlined such concepts as "bracing" the upper and lower body at address and "swinging inside a barrel," concepts that continue to resonate in golf instruction right through the present day. But his greatest and most enduring contributions may be those pertaining to the title of his book, the art of learning golf.

"Don't go out to find out what is wrong with your swing, go out to improve it," Boomer advised. "You will be none the worse if you start with a really big idea—to learn (or relearn) the golf swing at your first try. If that is your ambition, do not tie yourself up with theories; stand up and give the ball a crack—that is the most positive thing in golf."

An admirer of Walter Hagen's confidently relaxed attitude toward playing golf, Boomer emphasized the notion of "remembered feel" in teaching the physical aspects of the game. He tried to show his students how to shut out their "mental machinery" so they could focus instead on the "cycle of sensations" involved in swinging a club. "I say a golfer can only produce his true quality," Boomer declared, "when he can play *without* concentrating . . . when he can learn to make his shots without clenching his teeth."

Boomer's insights into the learning process are echoed by modern-day top-ten teaching pro Jim Flick, who has identified three developmental stages every golfer must go through to fulfill his potential. Stage one is "unconscious incompetence." That's when you're a novice who doesn't know what he is supposed to do and doesn't do what he does very well. Stage two is "conscious competence." That's when you know and think about what you're supposed to do and do it fairly well, though not to your full potential. Stage three is "unconscious competence." That's when you play to your full potential without having to think about it, or in Boomer's words, *"without* concentrating" or "clenching your teeth."

So how do you go about seeking and finding the best golf instruction, the kind that can help you take your game all the way to the stage of unconscious competence?

As the opening chapter of this book discusses in detail, the answer depends in large measure on who you are and what golfing

goals you have set for yourself, as defined by your golf instruction profile scorecard (GIPS). The best instruction is not the same for everybody. The best instruction is what is best for you.

Remember, there are two main types of golf instruction, error correction and swing development. You may be able to get a quick fix for a specific problem in a large number of places from a wide variety of instructors. But you are still likely to be better off if you follow the same approach recommended for golfers interested in a long-term swing development program. Even quick fixes and casual tips are more effective if they are offered by an instructor in the context of a specific method or approach.

Ideally, you should follow a three-step process in seeking and finding the instruction that is best for you. Step one is making a serious long-term commitment to improving your game, recognizing all that will entail. Step two is picking a teaching pro who advocates the putting, full-swing, and short-game methods you want to emulate. Step three is honoring your commitments to your teaching pro and to yourself.

Committing Yourself to Improvement

No long-term commitment in life should be taken lightly. That is true whether we are talking about marriage, or making a long-term commitment to improve your golf game. As one of the characters in

Michael Murphy's *Golf in the Kingdom* points out, golf and marriage are, in fact, very much alike. In addition to commitment, both require love, trust, faith, understanding, perseverance, and work. And the work involved must be a true labor of love, or there will be no joy or purpose in the pursuit.

In his book *The Golf of Your Dreams*, the sports psychologist Dr. Bob Rotella maintains that before you can commit to a serious plan to improve your game, you must admit to yourself "that you want to be good and that you have the talent to play well." The key words here are "talent" and "play well." The latter is a relative term. For a beginner, playing well might mean breaking 100. For an average golfer, it might mean breaking 80. For a more advanced player, it might mean shooting par or better.

In every case, talent is a major factor in the equation. Talent does not necessarily mean having the physical and mental gifts of Tiger Woods, though if your sights are set on winning major championships, those attributes would sure come in handy. According to Rotella, "Real talent is patience. It's persistence. It's the ability always to keep in mind the vision of yourself as you want to be." By that definition, quite a few people, including but by no means limited to Woods, have real talent. You have to decide if you're one of them.

But there are also several other important factors to consider, chief among them the time that it will take for you to improve your game enough to "play well." If you're a beginner and your goal is to

play well enough to have a legitimate scratch handicap, you're probably going to need at least three to five years. And that's assuming you're able to pursue your goal pretty much full-time. Some junior golfers have that kind of time, thanks to support from parents or guardians. Few adults enjoy the same luxury. Even if you're already an average golfer who wants to break 80 or a low handicapper who wants to shoot par or better, you're probably going to need at least a year, maybe two or three years, to reach your goal.

In any event, seriously trying to improve your game is going to require an extensive commitment of time over a long period of time, regardless of how much talent you possess or your personal definition of what it means to play well.

Money is another factor. How much money you'll need to spend to improve your game is an open-ended question. It depends on who you are, where you play, and how much you need to play to reach your goal. At most public and private courses you can practice your putting and certain aspects of your short game for free. But range balls cost money, and so do greens fees, club memberships, tournament entry fees, and first-rate equipment.

The single most important ingredient in your recipe for improvement—taking golf lessons—also costs money. As noted in the opening chapter, some of the top-ranked teaching pros such as Butch Harmon charge as much as $500 per hour for private sessions. It should also be noted, however, that many other first-rate

teaching pros charge considerably less than that. Veteran top-ten instructor Bob Toski charges $150 per hour; Michael Hebron, ranked twelfth in the *Golf Digest* poll of teaching pros, charges $130 per hour.

As Rotella points out, a good teaching pro is where you find him. The instructor who is best for you may not necessarily be the highest ranked in a magazine poll or the most expensive. Happily, teaching golf is a true labor of love for virtually all the best instructors, so if you have the patience to hang around their teaching facilities long enough, they are likely to offer you some valuable advice on an informal basis. But don't expect to be offered a formal improvement program or a series of lessons free of charge.

The bottom line is that even though you can't buy a better golf game like you might buy a better car, you can't reasonably expect to improve your golf game in a significant way without spending what most people would consider to be a significant amount of money.

Picking a Pro

Once you've resolved to improve your golf game, you must make a long-term commitment to a particular golf instructor who can lead you through the learning process. Just as we have compared golf and marriage, we have previously compared picking a teaching pro to picking a spouse and picking a putter. Without overdoing these analogies, suffice it to say that choosing the person with the potential

to help you make your golfing dreams come true is a highly personal matter. But there are also several general guidelines worth following.

The first step in finding the golf instructor who is best for you is to do some background research on the prospective candidates. The opening chapter of this book offered a composite list of eighteen questions a teaching pro should ask you and you should ask yourself before taking a lesson. Here is a list of eighteen questions you should ask a pro before taking a lesson, which cover such areas as the pro's own golfing background and competitive experience; his teaching philosophy, teaching experience, and the mentors who taught him; the full-swing, putting, and short-game methods he advocates; the type of program he recommends for improving your game; and what he intends to charge you for lessons.

Eighteen Questions to Ask a Pro Before Taking a Lesson

1   How long have you been playing golf and teaching golf?

2   Who taught you to play?

3   What important amateur/professional tournaments have you competed in?

4   What made you decide to become a teaching pro?

5   What other teaching pros are or have been your most influential mentors?

6 What types of golfers do you prefer to teach?

7 What full-swing method do you teach?

8 What putting method do you teach?

9 What short-game method do you teach?

10 What do you charge for lessons?

11 Do you plan to stay in this area for the foreseeable future?

12 What is your teaching philosophy?

13 Are you a "technical" teacher or a "feel" teacher?

14 Can you take a golfer with my present playing ability to the next level?

15 How long do you expect it will take me to reach my goal?

16 How often do you want me to take lessons?

17 How often do you want me to practice?

18 How often do you want me to play golf?

This questionnaire should serve merely as a starting point in your search for an instructor. There are numerous key considerations that cannot be properly asked or answered by means of a questionnaire. One of them is the pro's genuine desire and willingness to help

you improve your game. If you ask whether he can take a player of your ability to the next level, he will more than likely reply in the affirmative. But does he really want to? Can he really give you the time and attention you'll need? Does he plan to remain in the same location for the likely duration of your improvement program? Or does he have ambitions of moving on to another location or another job?

Another key consideration is the pro's teaching style, especially as it relates to your preferred style of learning. Certain instructors are extremely technical in their approach to golf. Some prefer to use visual images rather than verbal cues. Others prefer to teach by feel. Many of the top-ranked teachers combine a variety of approaches. Jim McLean, for example, uses a four-pronged educational approach. He tells you what he wants you to do (verbal). He demonstrates what he wants you to do (visual). He guides you through the motions he wants you to perform (feel). Then he prescribes some drills designed to help you incorporate what he wants you to do into your swing (repetition.)

Teaching the Game of Golf, the PGA of America's manual for specialty certification in the field of instruction, identifies several commonly encountered types of learning styles, one or more of which may match your own. For example, there are "left brain" learners who prefer highly logical, detailed approaches involving step-by-step thinking often communicated orally or in writing; these types of golfers enjoy drills. There are "right brain" learners who prefer to see, feel, and/or intuit the big picture without much verbal

instruction; these types of golfers prefer to play the game rather than perform drills.

A slightly different but related classification of learning styles distinguishes between "innovative" learners, who use their imaginations to relate new information to past personal experiences; "common sense" learners, who relate to realistic examples; "dynamic" learners, who relate to involvement in specific experiences; and "analytical" learners, who want to grasp underlying principles and concepts. Like the left brain and right brain learning types, all four of these learning styles require input, information processing, performance experience, and feedback.

The underlying issue here is communication. For you to learn golf effectively, the communication must be two-way. Can the pro get his instructional messages across to you in an effective manner? Can you get your feedback messages across to him? And if so, does he listen attentively and respond appropriately?

Then there is the issue of fun. Does your prospective instructor take genuine joy in teaching? Does he enjoy being around you? Do you enjoy being around him? Improving your golf game is going to require long hours on the practice range and out on the golf course. Will both of you look forward to these sessions? Or will both of you dread each encounter?

Finally, there is the issue of trust, the most important consideration of all. Your prospective instructor may have an impressive

résumé. He may be an accomplished player. He may even have taught some of the leading money winners on the PGA Tour. He may be a smooth and effective communicator. He may take pride and joy in teaching. But do you have faith in him and his approach to improving your golf game? When the going gets tough, as it inevitably will, do you feel that you can rely on him? Do you feel that he will always do what's in your best interests as a golfer and as a person?

For better or worse, there is really no way for you to research issues of trust, joy, communication, and desire other than by trial and error. It could be that you find the teaching pro that is best for you by blind luck or coincidence. But it is more likely, as well as highly recommended, that you try out two or three different instructors before settling on one particular pro. Chances are you can quickly narrow down your prospective choices on the basis of their preferred putting, full-swing, and short-game methods and their proximity to where you live. Take a couple of lessons from the leading candidates, and get a feel for each of them. Then take a tip from Allen Doyle, and let yourself be guided by your heart, your head, and your hands.

Honoring Your Commitments

One of the hardest things to do in life is not making a commitment but honoring it. And yes, the golf and marriage analogy applies here, too. It's fine to look around during the research stage described above. But

when that's done, it's done. The worst thing you can do is to keep flitting back and forth from one teaching pro to another, especially if they happen to teach with different styles or advocate different putting, full-swing, and short-game methods. Instead of making improvements, you'll only make yourself more frustrated and confused.

Once you've committed to a long-term improvement program and picked a pro you believe can help you take your game to the next level, you must resolve to stick with your program and your pro.

If you have picked a competent and trustworthy instructor, he should be able to prescribe a comprehensive, well-balanced improvement program for you. Ideally, it should cover every facet of the game, including the full swing, putting, the short game, and course management techniques. But don't be shy about consulting a specialist in one of those areas if you and your chosen pro conclude that you could benefit from outside expertise. The same applies if you need help with an emotional management problem. Most teaching pros are not sports psychologists, but they are usually happy to refer you to one if need be.

In order to honor your commitment, you must be prepared to do three things: take lessons, practice, and play. You will get best results if you do all three with your short-term and long-term goals in mind. When you are taking lessons and practicing, you are in what Rotella calls the "training mode." You are training your mind and body to make changes, to perform actions that will probably feel

awkward when you first try them, and continue to feel that way for weeks or months to come. But that's what taking lessons and practicing are for. When you go out to play, you must put yourself in the "trusting mode." You must trust that the lessons you've been taking and the practicing you've been doing will eventually pay off. But most of all, you must trust your swing and let yourself put it to the test out on the golf course so it has a chance to improve under actual playing conditions.

Dr. Rick Jensen, director of sports psychology at the Academy of Golf at PGA National in Palm Beach Gardens, Florida, outlines a three-phase process that marries elements of Flick's developmental path from "unconscious incompetence" to "unconscious competence," and Rotella's training/trusting modes. He calls the first phase the "conceptualization stage," during which you are trying to develop clear concepts of what the swing motions you are learning should look and feel like. Here it is important to heed the axiom "practice with a purpose." As Jensen tells his seminar audiences, "If a player doesn't understand the purpose for swinging the club in a certain way, learning will be inhibited."

The second phase is the "acquisition stage," during which you are attempting to master new technical positions or movements in your golf swing through repetition, typically in the form of hitting hundreds of balls on the practice range. Jensen points out that there is a tendency to focus on two things at once in a "split attention"

mind-set: (1) the new positions or movements; and (2) hitting the ball straight. He warns that if you overly dwell on hitting the ball straight, you may never change your swing. This is where your chosen instructor can be of invaluable help by gently but firmly redirecting your focus, and by pointing out whether or not the shots you are hitting off-line actually indicate that you're making the desired swing changes.

The third phase is the "transfer stage," during which you learn to take the new swing you've acquired on the lesson tee and in practice sessions out on the golf course. Here it is vital for you to play the course with the intention of hitting the new ball flight produced by your swing change, even if that ball flight is not always straight in the early going. "Keep in mind, an improved golf swing does not necessarily equate to a 'straight' ball flight," Jensen advises. "Ask your pro what ball flight you can expect after making a swing change." The first sign you've completed the "transfer stage" comes when you can swing the club with the intent of hitting an expected ball flight without worrying about technical positions. Then you can begin focusing on hitting the ball to your chosen targets and on playing the game.

Another way to help yourself honor your commitment to improvement is by keeping a journal that documents your lessons, practice sessions, and each round you play out on the golf course. You should also take full advantage of the latest technology by maintaining a library of the videotapes your pro makes of you and you

make of yourself. The journal and the videotapes will provide both a subjective and an objective record of your learning experiences. You'll be able to chart your progress and determine whether you are actually making positive forward strides during times when you might think you are not.

Just as important, keeping a journal and a library of videotapes can improve your ability to deal with making changes in your golf game. If you really want to improve, making changes is inevitable. But changes are almost always disorienting and discomforting. And to make significant changes, you often have to exaggerate the feel. What's more, as Jimmy Ballard points out, "feels can fool you."

Even great players seldom do what they feel like they do (or say they do) when making a swing change. When Tom Kite won the 1992 U.S. Open, he felt like he was picking the club straight up on his backswing and swinging at his left knee on his downswing because he had recently changed from the flat swing he had used all his career to a more upright motion with the help of Jim McLean. But the television tapes of Kite's consistently "on plane" swing in the Open showed otherwise. You may feel that you've shortened your backswing by two feet when you've actually shortened it by only a few inches. Keeping records will enable you to accurately gauge the changes you've made and the changes you still need to make.

You must also appreciate the fact that you are undertaking one of the greatest challenges in life. Improvement in your game will

not come overnight, nor will it come easily to most golfers. There will be times when you feel like you are not making any forward progress at all, times when you feel like you are actually going backward. But you can help yourself through those valleys and plateaus by remembering that you are committing to a long-term process, not merely seeking an immediate result, and that many great players before you have encountered the same obstacles.

"Golf is a game that must always be uncertain," Bobby Jones observed in *On Golf*. "I don't believe that anyone will ever master it to the extent that several have mastered billiards and chess. If someone should do so, I think he would give up—but that is a danger most of us would be willing to risk."

Last but by no means least, you will dramatically improve your ability to improve if you always keep sight of the fact that the game of golf is just that—a game. Tiger Woods's coach, Butch Harmon, takes notorious delight in playing games with and simply clowning around with his star pupil; he takes the same basic approach with the high handicappers who attend his golf schools. "The more fun you have, the more relaxed you're going to be," Harmon says. "And the more relaxed you are, the easier it's going to be for you to learn and get better."

To paraphrase Percy Boomer, the real secret to producing your true quality as a golfer is to learn how to learn (or relearn) the game

without clenching your teeth. The hope of playing better than we played the last time out is what keeps all of us coming back for more. But you will increase your chances of playing better if you go out on the lesson tee, the practice tee, and the golf course with a smile on your face, and let your heart, your head, and your hands simply have fun.

SUMMARY: *Seeking and Finding the Best Instruction for You*

▶STEP 1: MAKE A SERIOUS LONG-TERM COMMITMENT TO IMPROVING YOUR GAME, RECOGNIZING ALL THAT WILL ENTAIL.

To reach your true quality as a golfer, you will have to go through three developmental stages in the learning process, which can be described as the transition from "unconscious incompetence" through "conscious competence" to "unconscious competence." Be prepared to make an extensive commitment of time over a long period of time. Be aware that you can't reasonably expect to improve your game in a significant way without spending what most people would consider to be a significant amount of money.

STEP 2: PICK A TEACHING PRO WHO ADVOCATES THE PUTTING, FULL-SWING, AND SHORT-GAME METHODS YOU WANT TO EMULATE.

Do background research on at least two or three prospective candidates. Use the eighteen questions you should ask before taking a lesson as a starting point. But also be sure to research issues that cannot be answered by the questionnaire, such as the pro's desire to help you, his communication skills, his joy and love for the game, and his trustworthiness.

STEP 3: HONOR YOUR COMMITMENTS TO YOUR PRO AND YOURSELF.

Once you've committed to improve you game, you must resolve to stick with your program and your chosen teaching pro. Be prepared to take lessons, practice, and play. Be aware that you are undertaking a great challenge, and the improvement will not come easy or overnight.

▶Step 4: Have fun.

Remember, golf is supposed to be fun. As Percy Boomer might have put it, the real secret to producing your true quality as a golfer is to learn how to learn—or relearn—the game without clenching your teeth. Take a tip from Tiger Woods's coach, Butch Harmon. You'll learn faster and easier if you let yourself relax and have fun on the lesson tee, the practice tee, and out on the course.

APPENDIX A:
America's Top-Ranked Golf Instructors

The following list of America's leading golf instructors includes the top-ten-ranked teaching pros as selected in a poll of their peers conducted by *Golf Digest* in 2000, and various other distinguished teaching pros and sports psychologists whose insights contributed to the material contained in this book. The profiles are based on the author's firsthand experience, research of primary and secondary sources, and interviews with the teaching pros and their present and former students. For additional references, the reader is advised to consult the August 2000 and August 2001 issues of *Golf Digest* and the February 2001 issue of *Golf Magazine,* which offer listings of more than 400 instructors nationwide.

The Top Ten Teaching Pros

1. David Leadbetter

South African native Leadbetter gained initial fame in the late 1980s for revamping the swing of star pupil Nick Faldo, who went on to win three Masters and three British Opens. Other students have included Ernie Els, Nick Price, LPGA star Se Ri Pak, and junior golf prodigies Aree and Naree Wonglukliet. One of the leading advocates of the big-muscle swing method, Leadbetter emphasizes body and club positioning in a system that features eleven swing "links" and fifteen "athletic keys." Despite the complexity of his method, Leadbetter is praised for the precision of his teaching approach and for having one of the most acute analytical minds in the profession.

Locations: Champions Gate Resort, Davenport, FL (headquarters); twelve satellite academies in Florida, New York, Jamaica, Austria, France, Spain, England, Germany, Portugal, Thailand, Japan, and Switzerland.

Resort Affiliation: Champions Gate Resort.

Rates: Individual private lessons, $5,000 for a four-hour minimum; three-day golf schools $2,400.

Phone: 888-633-5323

2. Claude "Butch" Harmon Jr.

Harmon is the scion of a renowned family of golf instructors, including brothers Craig, Dick, and Bill, and late father Claude Harmon Sr., winner of the 1948 Masters. Best known for coaching Tiger Woods, who first came to him at age seventeen, Harmon formerly coached Greg Norman and Davis Love III. A former PGA Tour player and gifted storyteller, he advocates a mixed-muscle swing method, but treats each golfer as unique, and emphasizes "motion thoughts" rather than mechanics or body and club positioning. He also teaches creative short-game techniques such as the three-wood chip. Fans say that Harmon has inherited his father's observational genius, a gift peers refer to as "the eye," and that his unique experiences with Woods et al. make him an ideal coach for tour pros.

Locations: Butch Harmon School of Golf, Rio Secco Golf Club, Henderson, NV (headquarters); Vilamoura Golf Club, Vilamoura, Portugal; Our Lucaya Beach and Golf Resort, Grand Bahama Island, Bahamas

Resort Affiliation: Rio Hotel, Las Vegas, NV.

Rates: Individual private lessons, $500 per hour; three-day golf schools with hotel accommodations, $4,500.

Phone: 888-867-3226

3. Jim McLean

A former college All-American who played on the University of Houston team with future PGA Tour star Bruce Lietzke, McLean has coached the likes of 1992 U.S. Open champion Tom Kite, former Ryder Cupper Brad Faxon, and LPGA standout Cristie Kerr. His own mentors include Ken Venturi and the late Claude Harmon Sr. An advocate of big-muscle swing methods,

McLean emphasizes staying within specified "corridors of success" rather than attempting perfect positioning. One of his central tenets is the "25 percent" theory, which gives equal weight to the long game, the short game, course management, and mental/emotional management. McLean's fans praise the comprehensiveness and flexibility of his approach to teaching, and his ability to improve the games of average golfers.

Locations: Doral Golf Resort and Spa, Miami, FL (headquarters); Weston Hills Country Club, Weston, FL; PGA West, La Quinta, CA; La Quinta Resort & Club, La Quinta, CA; Grand Traverse Resort, Williamsburg, MI; Mariners Point Links and Practice Center, Foster, CA.

Resort Affiliations: Doral Golf Resort and Spa; PGA West; Grand Traverse Resort.

Rates: Individual private lessons, $375 per hour; three-day golf schools, $2,215 (tuition only; room and board varies by location).

Phone: 800-723-6725

4. Hank Haney

A veteran teaching pro with more than two decades of experience, Haney earned international recognition in 1998 thanks to star pupil Mark O'Meara, who won that year's Masters and British Open titles. Like his philosophical mentor John Jacobs, he uses a student's ball flight as the starting point of his analysis, and sees improving that ball flight as the ultimate goal of his instruction. Haney generally emphasizes small-muscle (hands and arms) techniques with average golfers and big-muscle (body) techniques with advanced players. Haney's admirers praise his technical knowledge and candid opinions.

Location: Hank Haney Golf Ranch, McKinney, TX.

Resort Affiliation: None, but rooms available at Hank Haney Golf Ranch.

Rates: Individual private lessons, $360 per hour.

Phone: 972-542-8800

5. Rick Smith

Smith is both an accomplished golf architect and an accomplished golf instructor whose star pupils include results-oriented PGA Tour players Phil Mickelson, Lee Janzen, Rocco Mediate, and Vijay Singh. In contrast to teachers who begin with the setup and work forward, Smith typically starts with the moment of impact and works backward. Admittedly eclectic in his approach, he believes that it is crucial for students to understand the roles of both the small muscles and the big muscles in their golf swings. His overall emphasis is on the concept of "matching" the functions of these two muscle groups. He typically prescribes drills using impact bags and mirrors. Smith's fans praise his personable teaching style and his relative lack of emphasis on complex swing mechanics.

Locations: Rick Smith Golf Academy, Sylvan Treetops Resort, Gaylord, MI (headquarters); Tiburon Golf Club, Naples, FL; Turning Stone Casino, Verona, NY.

Resort Affiliations: Sylvan Treetops Resort; Naples Ritz-Carlton; Turning Stone Casino.

Rates: Individual private lessons, $1,000 for two-hour minimum; three-day golf schools with hotel accommodations vary around $3,200.

Phone: 888-873-3677 (Michigan); 877-464-6531 (Florida); 315-361-7658 (New York)

6.Jim Flick

One of the deacons of American golf instruction, the septuagenarian Flick is among the leading advocates of the small-muscle swing method. Currently the coproprietor of the Nicklaus/Flick Game Improvement organization, he refined his teaching philosophy in golf schools geared to the mass market and in consultations with Jack Nicklaus. Flick's primary emphasis is on using the hands and arms both for control and for developing feel in the full swing and in the short game. He is also an accomplished trick-shot artist who can hit drives well over 200 yards while kneeling on a towel or sitting on a folding chair. Flick's fans praise his unflagging enthusiasm for teaching and his passion for the game of golf, as well as his special attentiveness to average and high-handicap golfers.

Locations: Desert Mountain Golf Club, Scottsdale, AZ (headquarters); Boca Raton Resort and Club, Boca Raton, FL; Naples Grande Golf Club, Naples, FL; Lake Las Vegas Resort, Henderson, NV; Superstition Mountain Golf Club, Phoenix, AZ; TPC at Sawgrass, Ponte Vedra, FL; Cabo del Sol Golf Club, Los Cabos, Mexico.

Resort Affiliations: Fairmont Scottsdale Princess (AZ); Boca Raton Resort and Club (FL); The Registry Resort (FL); Hyatt Regency Lake Las Vegas Resort (NV).

Rates: Individual private lessons, $300 per hour; three-day golf schools start at $2,495, not including hotel accommodations.

Phone: 800-642-5528

7. Dave Pelz

Pelz has built his reputation as an expert on putting and the short game. He is the only one of the top-ten-ranked golf instructors who does not teach the full swing. Pelz's students include PGA Tour and Senior PGA Tour stars Lee Janzen, Vijay Singh, Steve Elkington, Jesper Parnevik, Peter Jacobsen, Tom Kite, and Tom Jenkins. A former NASA researcher, Pelz played college golf at the University of Indiana. He is the leading advocate of the pure pendulum putting stroke and the multiple-swing approach to the short game, and the author of statistics-laden tomes such as *Dave Pelz's Putting Bible* and *Dave Pelz's Short Game Bible*. Pelz fans praise his "scientific" approach to golf instruction and the precision with which he defines his putting and short-game methods.

Locations: Dave Pelz Scoring Game School, Austin, TX (headquarters); Boca Raton Resort and Club, Boca Raton, FL; The Club at Cordillera, Edwards, CO; The Ranch at PGA West, La Quinta, CA; Pinehurst Golf Resort, Pinehurst, NC; and various traveling locations nationwide.

Resort Affiliations: Boca Raton Resort and Club (FL); PGA West (CA); The Lodge at Cordillera (CO); Pinehurst Resort (NC.).

Rates: Three-day scoring game schools start at $2,175, not including hotel accommodations; individual private lessons by appointment for negotiated fee (available only to graduates of scoring game school).

Phone: 800-833-7370

8. Chuck Cook

Cook is a disciple of the late Harvey Penick. He has worked with former Penick student Tom Kite, as well as with 1995 U.S. Open champion Corey Pavin and the late Payne Stewart, winner of two U.S. Opens and a PGA Championship. Cook founded his Academy of Golf in 1981, and claims that it was the first golf school to combine sports psychology and biomechanics with golf instruction. He insists that he is not a method teacher, and prides himself on striving for what he calls "balance" in swing mechanics and other aspects of the game with each student. Cook's fans note that he is the closest living instructional heir to Penick and praise him for his individually customized approach to instruction.

Location: Circle C Golf Club, Austin, TX

Rates: Individual private lessons, $175 per hour.

Phone: 512-330-0707

9. Bob Toski

Now in his middle seventies, Toski has the well-earned distinction of being the most accomplished player of all the nation's top-ten-ranked teaching pros. Back in 1954, he was the PGA Tour's leading money winner; four decades later, at age sixty-eight, he shot a 68 in a Senior PGA Tour event. Toski advocates a small-muscle swing method that relies on the hands and arms, but he differs from former colleagues like Jim Flick in according almost equal emphasis to the role of the knees and legs. Toski disciples praise him for his encyclopedic historical knowledge, his continuing ability to play the game, and his no-nonsense approach to teaching.

Location: Toski-Battersby Golf Learning Center, Coconut Creek, FL.

Rates: Individual private lessons, $150 per hour.

Phone: 954-975-2045

10. Jimmy Ballard

Ballard is the undisputed pioneer of modern big-muscle swing methods, which he developed under the tutelage of the late Sam Byrd, a former New York Yankees baseball player who went on to win twenty-nine tournaments as a professional golfer. Ballard described such key concepts as an "athletic" coil into the right side on the backswing and maintaining "connection" between the body and the hands and arms throughout the swing in his 1981 book *How to Perfect Your Golf Swing,* which appeared nearly ten years before David Leadbetter's emergence as the most publicly recognized advocate of big-muscle techniques. Ballard's present and former star pupils include Hal Sutton, Jim Colbert, Jesper Parnevik, Curtis Strange, Seve Ballesteros, Sandy Lyle, John Brodie, and Emilee Klein. Ballard fans praise him not only for the innovations he has pioneered but also for the simplicity and consistency of his approach to teaching over the years.

Locations: JB Golf Enterprises, Key Largo, FL; Family Golf Center, CB Smith Park, Fort Lauderdale, FL.

Rates: Individual private lessons, $250 per hour; full-day session $995; four-week players' school, $15,000, not including hotel accommodations.

Phone: 800-999-6664

Additional Names of Distinction
(in alphabetical order)

Mike Adams/Dr. Jim Suttie

Along with T. J. Tomasi, veteran teaching pros Adams and Suttie developed the LAWs of Golf system based on research into biomechanics. They place special emphasis on matching swing types to a golfer's body types, prescribing "leverage" techniques for average physiques, "arc" techniques for lanky, flexible physiques, and "width" techniques for short-armed, less flexible physiques. Fans claim that the LAWs of Golf offer a badly needed alternative to one-size-fits-all approaches.

Locations: Mike Adams, Trump International Golf Club, West Palm Beach, FL; Dr. Jim Suttie, Cog Hill Golf and Country Club, Lemont, IL.

Resort Affiliation: PGA National Golf Club, Palm Beach Gardens, FL.

Rates: Adams individual private lessons, $150 per hour; three-day golf schools, $1,095 plus tax, not including hotel accommodations. Suttie individual private lessons, $200 per hour; three-hour training session, $325.

Phone: 561-682-0700 (Adams); 630-257-5872 (Suttie)

Bruce Davidson

A native of Aberdeen, Scotland, Davidson recently became director of golf at River Oaks Country Club in Houston, where he was formerly an assistant to Dick Harmon. He takes pride in custom-tailoring his instruction, variously advocating elements of big-muscle and small-muscle methods depending on the needs of individual pupils. He also emphasizes "motion thoughts" and feels, believing that many contemporary teaching pros and their students have become overly dependent on frame-by-frame video-taped swing analysis. Davidson wins praise for his enthusiastic, personable style and his nontechnical approach to teaching.

Location: River Oaks Country Club, Houston, TX.

Rates: Individual lessons, $200 per hour.

Phone: 713-529-4321

Eben Dennis

Dennis grew up at Champions Golf Club in Houston, Texas, where he learned golf under the tutelage of club founders and former PGA Tour stars Jackie Burke and Jimmy Demaret. He played college golf at Florida State University and the University of St. Thomas in Houston. Following a battle with a debilitating back problem, Dennis developed an innovative method for teaching putting, the short game, and the full swing, inspired by the insights of Demaret. In contrast to most advocates of small-muscle methods, who place equal emphasis on the roles of the hands and arms, Dennis focuses primarily on the hands as the guiding force, with an athletically flexible body providing support. In the 2000 U.S. Open at Pebble Beach, his coaching helped Nick Faldo finish seventh overall and first in putts per

greens in regulation, ahead of tournament winner Tiger Woods. Beginners especially appreciate the relative simplicity of his "guiding hands" approach.

Location: Eben Dennis Golf Academy, Plano, TX.

Rates: Individual private lessons, $150 per hour.

Phone: 972-964-7676

Eden Foster

Foster is only in his middle thirties but has been teaching golf for nearly fifteen years at exclusive private clubs in New York, Connecticut, and Florida. Currently head professional at the Maidstone Club in East Hampton, Long Island, and Calusa Pines in Naples, Florida, he is a former college golfer and mini-tour player. Tabbed as an up-and-comer destined for inclusion among *Golf Magazine's* top one hundred teaching pros, Foster emphasizes "cause and effect" in his approach, especially when working with average golfers afflicted with chronic slices. Students praise his focus on fundamentals rather than quick-fix tips.

Locations: Maidstone Club, East Hampton, NY (April through October); Calusa Pines Golf Club, Naples, FL. (November through March).

Rates: Individual private lessons, $100 per hour; three-day golf schools, starting at $1,300, not including accommodations.

Phone: 561-819-0401

Dick Harmon

Although his older brother Butch has garnered greater notoriety for coaching Tiger Woods and Greg Norman, Harmon, who is ranked number twenty-two on the *Golf Digest* list of top teaching pros, has won deserved respect for his work with 1995 PGA Champion Steve Elkington and LPGA star Catrin Nilsmark. Like his father, the late Claude Harmon Sr., he is a master of all varieties of bunker shots. Like brother Butch, he takes a mixed-muscle approach to teaching the full swing, emphasizing the importance of matching body action with the actions of hands and arms. Few nonfamily members of the teaching profession rival his depth and breadth of experience.

Location: Houstonian Golf Club, Richmond, TX.

Resort Affiliation: The Houstonian, Houston, TX.

Rates: Individual private lessons, $250 per hour.

Phone: 713-819-7023

Michael Hebron

Ranked number twelve in the *Golf Digest* poll, Hebron advocates a big-muscle swing method and a "pure pendulum" putting stroke. He places special emphasis on the swing plane defined by the shaft angle of the golf club at address and on the importance of "compressing" the ball at impact by maintaining the forward-leaning angle of all clubs in the bag, including the putter. Hebron's admirers say he has an exceptional gift for communicating core knowledge of fundamentals.

Locations: Smithtown Landing Country Club, Smithtown, NY (summer); Palm Beach Polo and Country Club, Wellington, FL (winter).

Rates: Individual private lessons, $130 per hour; one-day workshop, $195

Phone: 631-979-6534

Dr. Rick Jensen

Jensen is director of sports psychology at the Academy of Golf at PGA National Resort and Spa in Palm Beach Gardens, Florida, and president of the Performance Enhancement Center in Boca Raton, Florida. He has worked with numerous PGA Tour, Senior PGA Tour, and LPGA Tour players, and provided performance-enhancement consulting for corporations such as Hewlett-Packard, Merrill Lynch, Ford Motor Company, Toshiba, and Nike. His approach blends elements of cognitive and behaviorist techniques. Jensen outlines a three-step process for learning golf that consists of a conceptualization stage, an acquisition stage, and a transfer stage. He is known for his personable style and easygoing sense of humor.

Contact Information: Dr. Jensen can be reached by phone at 561-852-3603.

Darrell Kestner

Ranked number twenty-seven in the *Golf Digest* poll, Kestner is accomplished both as a player and as a teaching pro. His victories include the 1996 PGA Club Professional Championship, the 1994 and 1995 New York State Opens, and the 1982, 1983, and 1997 Metropolitan Opens. Kestner's fans note that he is one of the best putters and putting instructors in the game.

Location: Deepdale Golf Club, Manhasset, NY.

Rates: Individual private lessons, $250 per hour.

Phone 516-365-9111

David Lee

Perennially on *Golf Magazine*'s list of top one hundred teaching pros, Lee is the father of the Gravity Golf system and one of the most proudly iconoclastic instructors in the business. The for-now version of the Gravity Golf swing is modeled on the swings of Fred Couples and the young Jack Nicklaus. The futuristic version eliminates a conventional backswing in favor of what Lee describes as a "referenced up route." Advocates of the Gravity Golf system claim it is a welcome alternative to traditional teaching.

Location: Gravity Golf School, Royal, AR.

Rates: Individual private lessons, $150 per hour, three-days golf schools $1,975, not including accommodations.

Phone: 800-444-2992

Dr. Phil Lee/Jeff Warne

Lee and Warne are coauthors of *Shrink Your Handicap,* a guide to emotional management and course management. Lee is a clinical instructor in psychiatry at Cornell University's Weill Medical College in New York City. Warne is a lead instructor at the Jim McLean Golf School at the Doral Golf Resort & Spa in Miami, Florida, and head professional at The Bridge in Noyac, New York. Lee is a pioneer in applying insights about the effects of anxiety-producing chemicals to golf, and in using a multidisciplinary methodology that customizes cognitive, insight-oriented, behavioral, and hypnotic approaches to the personalities and style of individual clients. The Lee-Warne book wins praise for its objectivity and comprehensiveness in examining a wide range of techniques applicable to the mental aspects of golf.

Contact information: Dr. Lee can be reached via e-mail at PhilLeeMD@aol.com; Warne can be reached by phone at 631-725-9805.

Dr. Ralph Mann/Fred Griffin

Mann, a former Olympic hurdler with a Ph.D. in biomechanics, and Griffin, a top-one-hundred teaching pro, developed the computer-generated graphic ModelPro swing based on films of more than one hundred top pros and statistical analysis. Proponents of the ModelPro claim it is a biomechanically perfect ideal that allows them to isolate the strengths and weaknesses of their own swings. The ModelPro swing can be viewed via the Internet, and individual comparisons can be made by submitting video tapes to Compusport.

Contact Information: ModelPro information can be obtained through Compusport, Pittsburgh, PA.

Phone: 212-281-9847, e-mail: info@modelgolf.com.

Locations: Grand Cypress Academy of Golf, One North Jacaranda, Orlando, FL; Robert Trent Jones Trail Academy of Golf, 167 SunBelt Parkway, Birmingham, AL.

Resort Affiliation: Grand Cypress Resort.

Rates: $245 for one-hour individual private lessons with Fred Griffin using ModelPro system at Grand Cypress; three-day golf schools vary by location.

Phone: 800-835-7377 for Grand Cypress Academy; 800-949-4444 for RTJ Trail.

Paul Marchand

Marchand played on the University of Houston golf team with Jim Nantz, Blaine McAlister, and Fred Couples. His most prominent students include Couples and Mike Donald, who lost a heartbreaking playoff to Hale Irwin

in the 1990 U.S. Open. A former assistant to Dick Harmon, Marchand is also an advocate of the mixed-muscle approach, emphasizing the importance of hand, arm, and body coordination in the golf swing. Ranked number forty-six on the *Golf Digest* list of top teaching pros, he is praised for his depth of knowledge and his disdain for quick-fix swing cures.

Location: Shadow Hawk Golf Club, Richmond, TX.

Resort Affiliation: The Houstonian, Houston, TX.

Rates: Individual private lessons, $250 per hour.

Phone: 281-340-7205

Rick Martino

Ranked number nineteen in the *Golf Digest* poll, Martino advocates a biomechanical approach to golf instruction. In addition to considering body type and physique, he emphasizes the importance of a student's capabilities in terms of overall physical motor skills, flexibility, mental perception, and rhythm. Martino gathers key data by means of a high-tech computerized motor assessment system that features sensors strapped to a student's chest and hips. Admirers say his approach is among the most scientific and nondogmatic.

Location: PGA Learning Center, Port St. Lucie, FL.

Resort Affiliation: PGA Village, Port St. Lucie, FL.

Rates: Individual private lessons, $100 per hour; three-day golf schools start at $895, not including hotel accommodations.

Phone: 561-468-7686

Dr. Bob Rotella

Rotella is the sports psychologist most widely consulted by professional and top-ranked amateur golfers. A former University of Virginia professor with a doctorate in education, he is also a low-handicap golfer. His list of present and former clients includes Lee Janzen, Tom Kite, Mark O'Meara, and many others. Rotella is the author of several best-selling books, including *Golf Is Not a Game of Perfect, Golf Is a Game of Confidence,* and *The Golf of Your Dreams*. Rotella's fans praise his straightforward, commonsense approach to sports psychology, which combines cognitive techniques, relaxation techniques, and self-hypnosis techniques.

Contact information: Dr. Rotella can be reached by phone at 804-296-8469.

Randy Smith

Ranked number twenty-eight on the *Golf Digest* list of top teaching pros, Smith is best known as the original mentor of 1997 British Open champion Justin Leonard, but he also works with PGA Tour pros Harrison Frazar and D. A. Weibring. Smith played on the golf team at Texas Tech, and later took about eight hours of lessons from the late Harvey Penick while honing his own teaching skills. He generally advocates a mixed-muscle approach to the full swing, and subscribes to the Penick philosophy that visual images are usually more effective than technical instruction. Students applaud his down-home style.

Location: Royal Oaks Country Club, Dallas, TX.

Rates: Individual private lessons, $90 for forty minutes.

Phone: 214-691-0339

Mitchell Spearman

Ranked among *Golf Magazine*'s top one hundred teaching pros, Spearman is a British-born former European PGA Tour player who served as David Leadbetter's top teaching assistant from 1988 to 1998. He has worked with numerous top tour pros, including Nick Faldo and Se Ri Pak. Now a solo practitioner, Spearman insists on giving one-on-one private lessons for a minimum of three hours in order to focus exclusively on each student. He emphasizes "sequencing," his term for moving the club, hands, arms, and body in the proper order during the swing. Fans claim his approach is much easier to learn than the positional approach favored by certain method teachers.

Locations: Manhattan Woods Golf Club, West Nyack, NY (April through October); other locations by appointment (November through March)

Rates: Individual private lessons only, $1,500 for a minimum three hours.

Phone: 212-579-8803

Ed Woronicz

Woronicz is director of golf operations and instruction for Natural Golf. A member of the PGA of America for over twenty years, he has also worked with big-muscle method pioneer Jimmy Ballard and small-muscle method advocate Bob Toski. Although he seldom teaches at present, Woronicz supervises and has helped train 150 instructors in the Natural Golf approach.

Locations: Hoffman Estates, IL (headquarters), plus 100 teaching sites around the U.S.

Rates: One-day schools, $349; three-day schools, $949 (not including accommodations).

Phone: 1-888-NAT-GOLF

APPENDIX B:
Eighteen Questions to Ask Yourself Before Taking a Lesson

1   How long have you been playing golf?

2   What is your present handicap?

3   What is the lowest your handicap has been?

4   What is your occupation?

5   How often do you practice and play golf?

6   How much money are you willing to spend on improving your game?

7   How much more time are you willing to spend on improving than you do now?

8   Are you looking to overhaul your golf game or simply to fix a specific fault?

9   What instructors and/or golf schools have you taken lessons from?

10 What are the strengths and weaknesses of your golf game?

11 What is your age?

12 Do you have any physical handicaps or injuries?

13 What is the state of your overall body flexibility and range of motion?

14 Do you have long, short, or average-length arms relative to your torso?

15 Do you tend to hit most shots to the left or to the right?

16 Do you stroke putts straight back and straight through or on an arc?

17 Do you consider yourself a "technical" player or a "feel" player?

18 What long-term and short term goals have you set for your golf game?

APPENDIX C:
Eighteen Questions to Ask a Pro Before Taking a Lesson

1   How long have you been playing golf and teaching golf?

2   Who taught you to play?

3   What important amateur/professional tournaments have you competed in?

4   What made you decide to become a teaching pro?

5   What other teaching pros are or have been your most influential mentors?

6   What types of golfers do you prefer to teach?

7   What full-swing method do you teach?

8   What putting method do you teach?

9   What short-game method do you teach?

10   What do you charge for lessons?

11   Do you plan to stay in this area for the foreseeable future?

12   What is your teaching philosophy?

13   Are you a "technical" teacher or a "feel" teacher?

14   Can you take a golfer with my present playing ability to the next level?

15   How long do you expect it will take me to reach my goal?

16   How often do you want me to take lessons?

17   How often do you want me to practice?

18   How often do you want me to play golf?

APPENDIX D:
Equipment and Club Fitting

One of the most common problems to plague average golfers is playing with clubs that do not properly fit them. In many cases, high or middle handicappers try to buy their way out of a swing flaw or a ball flight problem with clubs touted as "game improvement technology," only to find that their swing flaws and ball flight problems get worse instead of better. Teaching pros report, for example, that the typical male golfer afflicted with a chronic ballooning slice that costs him distance off the tee will often make a so-called macho mistake. In a misguided effort to hit the ball farther and lower, he discards his regular-shafted driver with 10 or 12 degrees of loft, and purchases a tour model driver with a stiff or even extra-stiff shaft that has only seven or eight degrees of loft. But rather than achieving the desired result, he ends up losing more distance and slicing the ball even more.

Modern club fitting is both an art and a science. The complexities and subtleties are such that most average golfers are best

advised to select clubs in consultation with a qualified teaching pro and/or a professional club fitter instead of simply buying clubs off the rack in a discount store or from an equipment catalog. But if you insist on fitting yourself, you can save yourself considerable time and money—and avoid unnecessary damage to your ego and your handicap—by heeding a few general principles regarding loft, lie angles, and shafts.

1. **Loft:** In the majority of cases, the higher the degree of loft, the better. This is especially true for average golfers when it comes to selecting drivers. To put it simply, loft produces backspin, and backspin helps balls fly straight as well as carry. Low-lofted drivers (i.e., those under 9 degrees) produce relatively little backspin, effectively magnifying hooks and slices.

2. **Lie angles:** The "standard" lie angles differ significantly from one club manufacturer to the next, and teaching pros differ in their prescriptions for individual students. Club fitters typically recommend that taller golfers use irons with more "upright" lie angles, and that shorter golfers use irons with "flatter" lie angles. But be aware that upright clubs can also promote draws and hooks, while flat clubs can promote fades and slices.

3. Shaft flex: The key considerations in choosing shafts for your clubs are your tempo and your swing speed. In general, the faster your tempo and swing speed, the stiffer your shaft should be. The slower your tempo and swing speed, the more flexible your shaft should be. Tour pros have swing speeds with their drivers that range from about 110 m.p.h. up to 140 m.p.h. Average golfers have swings speeds around 85 to 90 m.p.h. But be aware that a shaft that is too flexible can magnify hooks, and a shaft that is too stiff can magnify slices.

SOURCES

The books cited below served as the primary printed sources of the factual and background material used in this book. They are also recommended to readers interested in obtaining additional information on particular subjects related to putting, full swings, short game techniques, course management, and sports psychology.

Adams, Mike, T. J. Tomasi, and Jim Suttie. *The LAWs of the Golf Swing: Body-Type Your Swing and Master Your Game.* Harper Collins, 1998.

Adams, Mike, and T. J. Tomasi. *Play Better Golf.* Journey Editions, 1996.

Armour, Tommy. *Classic Golf Tips.* Tribune Publishing, 1995.

Aultman, Dick, and Ken Bowden. *The Methods of Golf's Masters: How They Played and What You Can Learn from Them.* Da Capo Press, 1975.

Ballard, Jimmy, with Brennan Quinn. *How to Perfect Your Golf Swing: Using "Connection" and the Seven Common Denominators.* NYT Special Services, 1981.

Boomer, Percy. *On Learning Golf.* Alfred A. Knopf, 1994.

Boros, Julius. *Swing Easy, Hit Hard: Tips from a Master of the Classic Golf Swing.* Harper Collins, 1965.

Cochran, Alastair, and John Stobbs. *Search for the Perfect Golf Swing: The Proven Scientific Approach to Fundamentally Improving Your Game.* Triumph Books, 1986.

Cook, Chuck, with Roger Schiffman. *Perfectly Balanced Golf: Your Key to a Winning Game.* Doubleday, 1997.

Faldo, Nick, with Richard Simmons. *A Swing for Life: How to Play the Faldo Way.* Penguin Books, 1995.

Farnsworth, Dr. Craig L. *See It and Sink It: Mastering Putting Through Peak Visual Performance.* Harper Collins, 1997.

Flick, Jim, with Glen Waggoner. *On Golf: Lessons from America's Master Teacher.* Villard Books, 1997.

Floyd, Ray, with Larry Dennis. *From 60 Yards In: How to Master Golf's Short Game.* Harper Collins, 1989.

Grimsley, Will. *Golf: Its History, People, and Events.* Prentice-Hall, 1966.

Haney, Hank, with John Huggan. *The Only Golf Lesson You'll Ever Need.* Harper Collins, 1999.

Harmon, Claude "Butch" Jr., with John Andrisani. *Butch Harmon's Playing Lessons.* Simon & Schuster, 1998.

———. *The Four Cornerstones of Winning Golf.* Simon & Schuster, 1996.

Hogan, Ben. *Ben Hogan's Power Golf.* A. S. Barnes, 1948.

Hogan, Ben, with Herbert Warren Wind. *Five Lessons: The Modern Fundamentals of Golf.* Simon & Schuster, 1957.

Jacobs, John, with Ken Bowden. *The Golf Swing Simplified*. Buford Books, 1993.

Jones, Robert Trent Jr. *Golf by Design: How to Lower Your Score by Reading the Features of a Course*. Little Brown, 1993.

Jones, Robert Tyre (Bobby) Jones Jr. *Bobby Jones on Golf*. Doubleday, 1966.

Jones, Robert Tyre (Bobby) Jones Jr., and O. B. Keeler. *Down the Fairway*. Minton, Balch & Company, 1927.

Jorgensen, Theodore P. *The Physics of Golf*. Springer-Verlag, 1994.

Kelley, Homer. *The Golfing Machine*. Star Systems Press, 1969.

Leadbetter, David, with John Huggan. *The Golf Swing*. Harper Collins, 1990.

Leadbetter, David, with Lorne Rubenstein. *The Fundamentals of Hogan*. Sleeping Bear Press/Doubleday, 2000.

Leadbetter, David, with Richard Simmons. *Lessons from the Golf Greats*. Harper Collins, 1995.

Lee, Dr. Phil, and Jeff Warne. *Shrink Your Handicap: A Revolutionary Program from an Acclaimed Psychiatrist and a Top 100 Golf Instructor*. Hyperion, 2000.

Loehr, Dr. James E. *Mental Toughness Training for Sports: Achieving Athletic Excellence*. Penguin, 1986.

Loehr, Dr. James E., and Peter J. McLaughlin. *Mentally Tough: The Principles of Winning at Sports Applied to Winning in Business*. M. Evans & Co., 1986.

Mann, Dr. Ralph, and Fred Griffin, with Guy Yocum. *Swing Like a Pro: The Breakthrough Method of Perfecting Your Golf Swing*. Broadway Books, 1998.

Martens, Rainer, Robin S. Vealey, and Damon Burton. *Competitive Anxiety in Sport*. Human Kinetics Books, 1990.

McLean, Jim, with Larry Dennis. *Golf School: The Tuition-Free Tee-to-Green Curriculum from Golf's Finest High-End Academy*. Doubleday, 1999.

Miller, Johnny, et al. *Breaking 90 with Johnny Miller*. Callaway Editions, 2000.

McCord, Gary, with John Huggan. *Golf for Dummies*. IDG Books Worldwide, 1996.

Murphy, Michael. *Golf in the Kingdom*. Viking, 1972.

Nicklaus, Jack. *My 55 Ways to Lower Your Golf Score*. Simon & Schuster, 1962.

Nicklaus, Jack, with Ken Bowden. *Golf My Way*. Simon & Schuster, 1974.

Obitz, Harry, and Dick Farley. *Golf Magazine's Six Days to Better Golf*. Harper Collins, 1977.

Peck, M. Scott. *Golf and the Spirit: Lessons for the Journey*. Harmony Books, 1999.

Pelz, Dave, with James A. Frank. *Dave Pelz's Putting Bible*. Broadway Books, 2000.

————. *Dave Pelz's Short Game Bible*. Broadway Books, 1999.

Pelz, Dave, with Nick Mastroni. *Putt Like the Pros: Dave Pelz's Scientific Way to Improving Your Stroke, Reading Greens, and Lowering Your Score.* Harper Collins, 1989.

Penick, Harvey, with Bud Shrake. *Harvey Penick's Little Red Book: Lessons and Teachings from a Lifetime of Golf.* Simon & Schuster, 1992.

PGA of America members, including Jim Flick et al. *Teaching the Game of Golf: Specialty Certification Program Candidate Manual.* PGA of America, 1998.

Rotella, Dr. Bob, with Bob Cullen. *Golf Is a Game of Confidence.* Simon & Schuster, 1996.

——. *Golf Is Not a Game of Perfect.* Simon & Schuster, 1995.

——. *The Golf of Your Dreams.* Simon & Schuster, 1997.

Toski, Bob, and Davis Love Jr. with Robert Carney. *How to Feel a Real Golf Swing: Mind-Body Techniques from Two of Golf's Greatest Teachers.* NYT Special Services, 1988.

Vardon, Harry. *The Complete Golfer.* McClure, Phillips, 1905.

Watson, Tom, with Nick Seitz. *Tom Watson's Strategic Golf.* Pocket Books, 1993.

Wiren, Dr. Gary. *PGA Teaching Manual: The Art and Science of Golf Instruction.* PGA of America, 1990.

Woods, Earl, with Pete McDaniel. *Training a Tiger: A Father's Guide to Raising a Winner in Both Golf and Life.* Harper Collins, 1997.